PREFACE

It has been the ordinary practice of the French poets, to dedicate their works of this nature to their king; especially when they have had the least encouragement to it, by his approbation of them on the stage. But, I confess, I want the confidence to follow their example, though, perhaps, I have as specious pretences to it, for this piece, as any they can boast of; it having been owned in so particular a manner by his majesty, that he has graced it with the title of his play, and thereby rescued it from the severity (that I may not say malice) of its enemies. But though a character so high and undeserved has not raised in me the presumption to offer such a trifle to his most serious view, yet I will own the vanity to say, that after this glory which it has received from a sovereign prince, I could not send it to seek protection from any subject. Be this poem, then, sacred to him, without the tedious form of a dedication, and without presuming to interrupt those hours which he is daily giving to the peace and settlement of his people.

For what else concerns this play, I would tell the reader, that it is regular, according to the strictest of dramatic laws; but that it is a commendation which many of our poets now despise, and a beauty which our common audiences do not easily discern. Neither indeed do I value myself upon it; because, with all that symmetry of parts, it may want an air and spirit (which consists in the writing) to set it off. 'Tis a question variously disputed, whether an author may be allowed as a competent judge of his own works. As to the fabric and contrivance of them, certainly he may; for that is properly the employment of the judgment; which, as a master-builder, he may determine, and that without deception, whether the work be according to the exactness of the model; still granting him to have a perfect idea of that pattern by which he works, and that he keeps himself always constant to the discourse of his judgment, without admitting self-love, which is the false surveyor of his fancy, to intermeddle in it. These qualifications granted (being such as all sound poets are presupposed to have within them), I think all writers, of what kind soever, may infallibly judge of the frame and contexture of their works. But for the ornament of writing, which is greater, more various, and bizarre in poesy than in any other kind, as it is properly the child of fancy; so it can receive no measure, or at least but a very imperfect one, of its own excellences or failures from the judgment. Self-love (which enters but rarely into the offices of the judgment) here predominates; and fancy (if I may so speak), judging of itself, can be no more certain, or demonstrative of its own effects, than two crooked lines can be the adequate measure of each other. What I have said on this subject may, perhaps, give me some credit with my readers, in my opinion of this play, which I have ever valued above the rest of my follies of this kind; yet not thereby in the least dissenting from their judgment, who have concluded the writing of this to be much inferior to my "Indian Emperor." But the argument of that was much more noble, not having the allay of comedy to depress it; yet if this be more perfect, either in its kind, or in the general notion of a play, it is as much as I desire to have granted for the vindication of my opinion, and what as nearly touches me, the sentence of a royal judge. Many have imagined the character of Philocles to be faulty; some for not discovering the queen's love, others for his joining in her restraint: But though I am not of their number, who obstinately defend what they have once said, I may, with modesty, take up those answers which have been made for me by my friends; namely, that Philocles, who was but a gentleman of ordinary birth, had no reason to guess so soon at the queen's passion; she being a person so much above him, and, by the suffrages of all her people, already destined to Lysimantes: Besides, that he was prepossessed (as the queen somewhere hints it to him) with another inclination, which rendered him less clear-sighted in it, since no man, at the same time, can distinctly view two different objects; and if this, with any shew of reason, may be defended, I leave my masters, the critics, to determine, whether it be not much more conducing to the beauty of my plot, that Philocles should be long kept ignorant of the queen's love, than that with one leap he should have entered into the knowledge of it, and thereby freed himself, to the disgust of the audience, from that pleasing labyrinth of errors which was prepared for him. As for that other objection, of his joining in the queen's imprisonment, it is indisputably that which every man, if he examines himself, would have done on the like occasion. If they answer, that it takes from the height of his character to do it; I would enquire of my overwise censors, who told them I intended him a perfect character, or, indeed, what necessity was there he should be so, the variety of images being one great beauty of a play? It was as much as I designed, to shew one great and absolute pattern of honour in my poem, which I did in the person of the queen: all the defects of the other parts being set to shew, the more to recommend that one character of virtue to the audience. But neither was the fault of Philocles so great, if the circumstances be considered, which, as moral philosophy assures us, make the essential differences of good and bad; he himself best explaining his own intentions in his last act, which was the restoration of his queen; and even before that, in the honesty of his expressions, when he was unavoidably led by the impulsions of his love to do it. That which with more reason was objected as an indecorum, is the management of the last scene of the play, where Celadon and Florimel are treating too lightly of their marriage in the presence of the queen, who likewise seems to stand idle, while the great action of the drama is still depending. This I cannot otherwise defend, than by telling you, I so designed it on purpose, to make my play go off more smartly; that scene being, in the opinion of the best judges, the most divertising of the whole comedy. But though the artifice succeeded, I am willing to acknowledge it as a fault, since it pleased his majesty, the best judge, to think it so.

I have only to add, that the play is founded on a story in the "Cyrus," which he calls the Queen of Corinth; in whose character, as it has been affirmed to me, he represents that of the famous Christina, queen of Sweden. This is what I thought convenient to write by way of preface to "The Maiden Queen;" in the reading of which I fear you will not meet with that satisfaction, which you have had in seeing it on the stage; the chief parts of it, both serious and comic, being performed to that height of excellence, that nothing but a command, which I could not handsomely disobey, could have given me the courage to have made it public.

PROLOGUE

I.
He who writ this, not without pains and thought,
From French and English theatres has brought
The exactest rules, by which a play is wrought.

II.
The unities of action, place, and time;
The scenes unbroken; and a mingled chime
Of Jonson's humour, with Corneille's rhyme.

III.
But while dead colours he with care did lay,
He fears his wit, or plot, he did not weigh,
Which are the living beauties of a play.

IV.
Plays are like towns, which, howe'er fortified
By engineers, have still some weaker side,
By the o'er-seen defendant unespied.

V.

And with that art you make approaches now;
Such skilful fury in assaults you show,
That every poet without shame may bow.

VI.

Ours, therefore, humbly would attend your doom,
If, soldier-like, he may have terms to come,
With flying colours, and with beat of drum.

The Prologue goes out, and stays while a tune is played, after which he returns again.

SECOND PROLOGUE

I had forgot one half, I do protest,
And now am sent again to speak the rest.
He bows to every great and noble wit;
But to the little Hectors of the pit
Our poet's sturdy, and will not submit.
He'll be beforehand with 'em, and not stay
To see each peevish critic stab his play;
Each puny censor, who, his skill to boast,
Is cheaply witty on the poet's cost.
No critic's verdict should, of right, stand good,
They are excepted all, as men of blood;
And the same law shall shield him from their fury,
Which has excluded butchers from a jury.
You'd all be wits—
But writing's tedious, and that way may fail;
The most compendious method is to rail:
Which you so like, you think yourselves ill used,
When in smart prologues you are not abused.
A civil prologue is approved by no man;
You hate it, as you do a civil woman:
Your fancy's palled, and liberally you pay
To have it quickened ere you see a play;
Just as old sinners, worn from their delight,
Give money to be whipped to appetite.
But what a pox keep I so much ado
To save our poet? He is one of you;
A brother judgment, and, as I hear say,
A cursed critic as e'er damned a play.
Good savage gentlemen, your own kind spare;
He is, like you, a very wolf or bear;
Yet think not he'll your ancient rights invade,
Or stop the course of your free damning trade;
For he (he vows) at no friend's play can sit,
But he must needs find fault, to shew his wit:
Then, for his sake, ne'er stint your own delight;

Throw boldly, for he sits to all that write;
With such he ventures on an even lay,
For they bring ready money into play.
Those who write not, and yet all writers nick,
Are bankrupt gamesters, for they damn on tick.

LYSIMANTES, first Prince of the Blood.
PHILOCLES, the Queen's favourite.
CELADON, a courtier.
QUEEN of Sicily.
CANDIOPE, Princess of the Blood.
ASTERIA, the Queen's confident.
FLORIMEL, a maid of honour.
FLAVIA, another maid of honour.
OLINDA, SABINA, Sisters.
MELISSA, mother to OLINDA and SABINA.
Guards, Pages of Honour, Soldiers.

SCENE — Sicily

Vitiis nemo sine nascitur; optimus ille
Qui minimis urgetur.--HORAT.

This play is composed in a mixture of rhymed verse, blank verse, and prose.

ACT I

SCENE I—Walks near the Court.

Enter CELADON and ASTERIA, meeting each other, he in a riding habit; they embrace.

CELADON - Dear Asteria!—

ASTERIA - My dear brother, welcome! A thousand welcomes! Methinks, this year, you have been absent, has been so tedious:—I hope, as you have made a pleasant voyage, so you have brought your good humour back again to court?

CELADON - I never yet knew any company I could not be merry in, except it were an old woman's.

ASTERIA - Or at a funeral.

CELADON - Nay, for that you shall excuse me; for I was never merrier than I was at a creditor's of mine, whose book perished with him. But what new beauties have you at court? How do Melissa's two fair daughters?

ASTERIA - When you tell me which of them you are in love with, I'll answer you.

CELADON - Which of them, naughty sister! what a question's there? With both of them; with each and singular of them.

ASTERIA - Bless me!—You are not serious?

CELADON - You look, as if it were a wonder to see a man in love. Are they not handsome?

ASTERIA - Ay; but both together—

CELADON - Ay, and both asunder; why, I hope there are but two of them; the tall singing and dancing one, and the little innocent one?

ASTERIA - But you cannot marry both?

CELADON - No, nor either of them, I trust in Heaven: but I can keep them company; I can sing and dance with them, and treat them; and that, I take it, is somewhat better than musty marrying them. Marriage is poor folks' pleasure, that cannot go to the cost of variety; but I am out of danger of that with these two, for I love them so equally, I can never make choice between them. Had I but one mistress, I might go to her to be merry, and she, perhaps, be out of humour; there were a visit lost: But here, if one of them frown upon me, the other will be the more obliging, on purpose to recommend her own gaiety; besides a thousand things that I could name.

ASTERIA - And none of them to any purpose.

CELADON - Well, if you will not be cruel to a poor lover, you might oblige me, by carrying me to their lodgings.

ASTERIA - You know I am always busy about the queen.

CELADON - But once or twice only; 'till I am a little flushed in my acquaintance with other ladies, and have learned to prey for myself. I promise you I'll make all the haste I can to end the trouble, by being in love somewhere else.

ASTERIA - You would think it hard to be denied now?

CELADON - And reason good. Many a man hangs himself for the loss of one mistress: How do you think, then, I should bear the loss of two; especially in a court, where, I think, beauty is but thin sown?

ASTERIA - There's one Florimel, the queen's ward, a new beauty, as wild as you, and a vast fortune.

CELADON - I am for her before the world. Bring me to her, and I'll release you of your promise for the other two.

Enter a Page.

PAGE - Madam, the queen expects you.

CELADON - I see you hold her favour; adieu, sister:—you have a little emissary there, otherwise I would offer you my service.

ASTERIA - Farewell, brother; think upon Florimel.

CELADON - You may trust my memory for a handsome woman: I'll think upon her, and the rest too; I'll forget none of them.

[Exit ASTERIA.

SCENE II

Enter a Gentleman walking over the stage hastily; After him FLORIMEL and FLAVIA masked.

FLAVIA - Phormio! Phormio! you will not leave us?

GENTLEMAN - In faith, I have a little business.

[Exit GentLEMAN.

CELADON - Cannot I serve you in the gentleman's room, ladies?

FLAVIA - Which of us would you serve?

CELADON - Either of you, or both of you.

FLAVIA - Why, could you not be constant to one?

CELADON - Constant to one!—I have been a courtier, a soldier, and a traveller, to good purpose, if I must be constant to one: Give me some twenty, some forty, some a hundred mistresses! I have more love than any woman can turn her to.

FLORIMEL - Bless us! let us be gone, cousin: We two are nothing in his hands.

CELADON - Yet, for my part, I can live with as few mistresses as any man. I desire no superfluities; only for necessary change or so, as I shift my linen.

FLORIMEL - A pretty odd kind of fellow this; he fits my humour rarely. [Aside.

FLAVIA - You are as inconstant as the moon.

FLORIMEL - You wrong him, he's as constant as the sun; he would see all the world in twenty-four hours.

CELADON - 'Tis very true, madam; but, like him, I would visit, and away.

FLORIMEL - For what an unreasonable thing it were, to stay long, be troublesome, and hinder a lady of a fresh lover.

CELADON - A rare creature this! [Aside]—Besides, madam, how like a fool a man looks, when, after all his eagerness of two minutes before, he shrinks into a faint kiss, and a cold compliment. Ladies both, into your hands I commit myself; share me betwixt you.

FLAVIA - I'll have nothing to do with you, since you cannot be constant to one.

CELADON - Nay, rather than lose either of you, I'll do more; I'll be constant to an hundred of you. Or, if you will needs fetter me to one, agree the matter between yourselves; and the most handsome take me.

FLORIMEL - Though I am not she, yet since my mask is down, and you cannot convince me, have a good faith of my beauty, and for once I take you for my servant.

CELADON - And for once I'll make a blind bargain with you. Strike hands; is't a match, mistress?

FLORIMEL - Done, servant.

CELADON - Now I am sure I have the worst on't: For you see the worst of me, and that I do not of you, 'till you shew your face. Yet, now I think on't, you must be handsome.

FLORIMEL - What kind of beauty do you like?

CELADON - Just such a one as yours.

FLORIMEL - What's that?

CELADON - Such an oval face, clear skin, hazel eyes, thick brown eye-brows, and hair as you have, for all the world.

FLAVIA - But I can assure you, she has nothing of all this.

CELADON - Hold thy peace, envy; nay, I can be constant an I set on't.

FLORIMEL - 'Tis true she tells you.

CELADON - Ay, ay, you may slander yourself as you please: Then you have,—let me see.

FLORIMEL - Ill swear, you shall not see.

CELADON - A turned up nose, that gives an air to your face:—Oh, I find I am more and more in love with you!—a full nether lip, an out-mouth, that makes mine water at it; the bottom of your cheeks a little blub, and two dimples when you smile: For your stature, 'tis well; and for your wit, 'twas given you by one that knew it had been thrown away upon an ill face. Come, you're handsome, there's no denying it.

FLORIMEL - Can you settle your spirits to see an ugly face, and not be frighted? I could find in my heart to lift up my mask, and disabuse you.

CELADON - I defy your mask:—Would you would try the experiment!

FLORIMEL - No, I won't; for your ignorance is the mother of your devotion to me.

CELADON - Since you will not take the pains to convert me, I'll make bold to keep my faith. A miserable man, I am sure, you have made me.

FLAVIA - This is pleasant.

CELADON - It may be so to you, but it is not to me; for aught I see, I am going to be the most constant Maudlin,—

FLORIMEL - 'Tis very well, Celadon; you can be constant to one you have never seen, and have forsaken all you have seen?

CELADON - It seems, you know me then:—Well, if thou should'st prove one of my cast mistresses, I would use thee most damnably, for offering to make me love thee twice.

FLORIMEL - You are i'the right: An old mistress, or servant, is an old tune; the pleasure on't is past, when we have once learned it.

FLAVIA - But what woman in the world would you wish her like?

CELADON - I have heard of one Florimel, the queen's ward; would she were as like her for beauty, as she is for humour!

FLAVIA - Do you hear that, cousin? [To FLOR. aside.

FLORIMEL - Florimel's not handsome: Besides she's inconstant; and only loves for some few days.

CELADON - If she loves for shorter time than I, she must love by winter days and summer nights, i'faith.

FLORIMEL - When you see us together, you shall judge. In the mean time, adieu, sweet servant.

CELADON - Why, you won't be so inhuman to carry away my heart, and not so much as tell me where I may hear news on't?

FLORIMEL - I mean to keep it safe for you; for, if you had it, you would bestow it worse: Farewell, I must see a lady.

CELADON - So must I too, if I can pull off your mask.

FLORIMEL - You will not be so rude, I hope.

CELADON - By this light, but I will!

FLORIMEL - By this leg, but you shan't.

[Exeunt FLORIMEL - and FLAVIA - running.

SCENE III

Enter PHILOCLES, and meets him going out.

CELADON - How! my cousin, the new favourite!—[Aside.

PHILOCLES - Dear Celadon! most happily arrived.
I hear you've been an honour to your country
In the Calabrian wars; and I am glad
I have some interest in it.

CELADON - But in you
I have a larger subject for my joys:
To see so rare a thing as rising virtue,
And merit, understood at court.

PHILOCLES - Perhaps it is the only act, that can
Accuse our queen of weakness.

Enter LYSIMANTES, attended.

LYSIMANTES - O, my lord Philocles, well overtaken!
I came to look you.

PHILOCLES - Had I known it sooner,
My swift attendance, sir, had spared your trouble.
Cousin, you see prince Lysimantes [To CELADON.
Is pleased to favour me with his commands:
I beg you'll be no stranger now at court.

CELADON - So long as there be ladies there, you need
Not doubt me. [Exit CELADON.

PHILOCLES - Some of them will, I hope, make you a convert.

LYSIMANTES - My lord Philocles, I'm glad we are alone;
There is a business, that concerns me nearly,
In which I beg your love.

PHILOCLES - Command my service.

LYSIMANTES - I know your interest with the queen is great;
(I speak not this as envying your fortune,
For, frankly, I confess you have deserved it;
Besides, my birth, my courage, and my honour,
Are all above so base a vice,)—

PHILOCLES - I know, my lord, you are first prince o'the blood;
Your country's second hope:

And that the public vote, when the queen weds,
Designs you for her choice.

LYSIMANTES - I am not worthy,
Except love makes desert;
For doubtless she's the glory of her time:
Of faultless beauty, blooming as the spring
In our Sicilian groves; matchless in virtue,
And largely souled where'er her bounty gives,
As, with each breath, she could create new Indies.

PHILOCLES - But jealous of her glory,—

LYSIMANTES - You are a courtier; and, in other terms,
Would you say, she is averse from marriage,
Lest it might lessen her authority.
But whensoe'er she does, I know the people
Will scarcely suffer her to match
With any neighbouring prince, whose power might bend
Our free Sicilians to a foreign yoke.

PHILOCLES - I love too well my country to desire it.

LYSIMANTES - Then, to proceed, (as you well know, my lord,)
The provinces have sent their deputies,
Humbly to move her, she would chuse at home;
And, (for she seems averse from speaking with them,)
By my appointment, have designed these walks,
Where well she cannot shun them. Now, if you
Assist their suit, by joining yours to it,
And by your mediation I prove happy,
I freely promise you—

PHILOCLES - Without a bribe, command my utmost in it:—
And yet, there is a thing, which time may give me
The confidence to name,—

LYSIMANTES - 'Tis yours whatever:—
But, tell me true, does she not entertain
Some deep and settled thoughts against my person?

PHILOCLES - I hope, not so; but she, of late, is froward;
Reserved, and sad, and vexed at little things;
Which her great soul, ashamed of, strait shakes off,
And is composed again.

LYSIMANTES - You are still near the queen; and all our actions
Come to princes' eyes, as they are represented
By them, that hold the mirror.

PHILOCLES - Here she comes, and with her the deputies:

I fear all is not right.

Enter QUEEN, Deputies after her; ASTERIA, Guard, FLAVIA, OLINDA, and SABINA. Queen turns back to the Deputies, and speaks entering.

QUEEN - And I must tell you,
It is a saucy boldness, thus to press
On my retirements.

1ST DEPUTY - Our business being of no less concern,
Than is the peace and quiet of your subjects;—
And that delayed,—

2ND DEPUTY - We humbly took this time
To represent your people's fears to you.

QUEEN - My people's fears! who made them statesmen?
They much mistake their business, if they think,
It is to govern.
The rights of subjects, and of sovereigns,
Are things distinct in nature:—Theirs is to
Enjoy propriety, not empire.

LYSIMANTES - If they have erred, 'twas but an over-care;
An ill-timed duty.

QUEEN - Cousin, I expect
From your near blood, not to excuse, but check them.
They would impose a ruler upon their lawful queen:
For what's an husband else?

LYSIMANTES - Far, madam, be it from the thoughts
Of any, who pretends to that high honour,
To wish for more than to be reckoned
As the most graced, and first of all your servants.

QUEEN - These are the insinuating promises
Of those, who aim at power. But tell me, cousin,
(For you are unconcerned, and may be judge,)
Should that aspiring man compass his ends,
What pawn of his obedience could he give me,
When kingly power were once invested in him?

LYSIMANTES - What greater pledge than love! When those fair eyes
Cast their commanding beams, he, that could be
A rebel to your birth, must pay them homage.

QUEEEN - All eyes are fair,
That sparkle with the jewels of a crown:
But now I see my government is odious;
My people find I am not fit to reign,

Else they would never—

LYSIMANTES - So far from that, we all acknowledge you
The bounty of the gods to Sicily:
More than they are you cannot make our joys;
Make them but lasting in a successor.

PHILOCLES - Your people seek not to impose a prince;
But humbly offer one to your free choice:
And such a one he is—may I have leave
To speak some little of his great deserts?—

QUEEN - I'll hear no more.
For you, attend to-morrow at the council:
[To the Deputies.
There you shall have my firm resolves:—meantime,
My cousin, I am sure, will welcome you.

LYSIMANTES - Still more and more mysterious: But I have
Gained one of her women that shall unriddle it.
[Aside.
Come, gentlemen.

ALL deputies - Heaven preserve your majesty!

[Exeunt LYSIMANTES - and Deputies.

QUEEN - Philocles, you may stay.

PHILOCLES - I humbly wait your majesty's commands.

QUEEN - Yet, now I better think on't, you may go.

PHILOCLES - Madam!

QUEEN - I have no commands;—or, what's all one,
You, no obedience.

PHILOCLES - How! no obedience, madam?
I plead no other merit; 'tis the charter
By which I hold your favour, and my fortunes.

QUEEN - My favours are cheap blessings, like rain and sunshine,
For which we scarcely thank the gods, because
We daily have them.

PHILOCLES - Madam, your breath, which raised me from the dust,
May lay me there again:
But fate nor time can ever make me lose
The sense of your indulgent bounties to me.

QUEEN - You are above them now, grown popular:—
Ah, Philocles! could I expect from you
That usage!—no tongue but yours
To move me to a marriage?—[Weeps.
The factious deputies might have some end in't,
And my ambitious cousin gain a crown:
But what advantage could there come to you?
What could you hope from Lysimantes' reign,
That you can want in mine?

PHILOCLES - You yourself clear me, madam. Had I sought
More power, this marriage sure was not the way.
But, when your safety was in question,
When all your people were unsatisfied,
Desired a king,—nay more, designed the man,—
It was my duty then,—

QUEEN - Let me be judge of my own safety.
I am a woman;
But danger from my subjects cannot fright me.

PHILOCLES - But Lysimantes, madam, is a person,—

QUEEN - I cannot love.
Shall I,—I, who was born a sovereign queen,
Be barred of that, which God and nature gives
The meanest slave, a freedom in my love?—
Leave me, good Philocles, to my own thoughts;
When next I need your counsel, I'll send for you.

PHILOCLES - I'm most unhappy in your high displeasure;
But, since I must not speak, madam, be pleased
To peruse this, and therein read my care.

[He plucks out a paper, and presents it to her; but drops, unknown to him, a picture. Exit PHI.

QUEEN - [reads.] A catalogue of such persons,—
What's this he has let fall, Asteria?
[Spies the box.

ASTERIA - Your majesty?—

QUEEN - Take that up; it fell from Philocles.

[She takes it up, looks on it, and smiles.

QUEEN - How now, what makes you merry?

ASTERIA - A small discovery I have made, madam.

QUEEN - Of what?

ASTERIA - Since first your majesty graced Philocles,
I have not heard him named for any mistress,
But now this picture has convinced me.

QUEEN - Ha! let me see it.
[Snatches it from her.
Candiope, prince Lysimantes' sister!

ASTERIA - Your favour, madam, may encourage him,—
And yet he loves in a high place for him:
A princess of the blood; and, what is more,
Beyond comparison the fairest lady
Our isle can boast.

QUEEN - How!—she the fairest
Beyond comparison!—'Tis false! you flatter her;
She is not fair.

ASTERIA - I humbly beg forgiveness on my knees,
If I offended you:—But next yours, madam,
Which all must yield to.

QUEEN - I pretend to none.

ASTERIA - She passes for a beauty.

QUEEN - Ay, she may pass:—But why do I speak of her?—
Dear Asteria, lead me, I am not well o' the sudden.
[She faints.

ASTERIA - Who's near there?—help the queen!

[The guards are coming.

QUEEN - Bid them away: 'Twas but a qualm,
And 'tis already going.

ASTERIA - Dear madam, what's the matter?
You are of late so altered, I scarce know you.
You were gay humoured, and you now are pensive;
Once calm, and now unquiet:—
Pardon my boldness, that I press thus far
Into your secret thoughts: I have, at least,
A subject's share in you.

QUEEN - Thou hast a greater.
That of a friend:—But I am froward, say'st thou?

ASTERIA - It ill becomes me, madam, to say that.

QUEEN - I know I am:—Pr'ythee, forgive me for it,—
I cannot help it;—but thou hast
Not long to suffer it.

ASTERIA - Alas!

QUEEN - I feel my strength each day and hour consume,
Like lilies wasting in a lymbeck's heat.
Yet a few days,
And thou shalt see me lie, all damp and cold,
Shrouded within some hollow vault, among
My silent ancestors.

ASTERIA - O dearest madam!
Speak not of death; or think not, if you die,
That I will stay behind.

QUEEN - Thy love has moved me;—I, for once, will have
The pleasure to be pitied. I'll unfold
A thing so strange, so horrid of myself—

ASTERIA - Bless me, sweet heaven!—
So horrid, said you, madam?

QUEEN - That sun, who with one look surveys the globe,
Sees not a wretch like me!—And could the world
Take a right measure of my state within,
Mankind must either pity me, or scorn me.

ASTERIA - Sure none could do the last.

QUEEN - Thou longest to know it,
And I to tell thee, but shame stops my mouth.
First, promise me thou wilt excuse my folly;
And, next, be secret.

ASTERIA - Can you doubt it, madam?

QUEEN - Yet you might spare my labour:—
Can you not guess?

ASTERIA - Madam, please you, I'll try.

QUEEN - Hold, Asteria!—
I would not have you guess; for should you find it,
I should imagine that some other might,
And then I were most wretched:—
Therefore, though you should know it, flatter me,
And say you could not guess it.

ASTERIA - Madam, I need not flatter you, I cannot—and yet,

Might not ambition trouble your repose?

QUEEN - My Sicily, I thank the Gods, contents me.
But, since I must reveal it, know,—'tis love:
I, who pretended so to glory, am
Become the slave of love.

ASTERIA - I thought your majesty had framed designs
To subvert all your laws; become a tyrant,
Or vex your neighbours, with injurious wars;
Is this all, madam?

QUEEN - Is not this enough?
Then, know, I love below myself; a subject;
Love one, who loves another, and who knows not
That I love him.

ASTERIA - He must be told it, madam.

QUEEN - Not for the world, Asteria:
Whene'er he knows it, I shall die for shame.

ASTERIA - What is it, then, that would content you?

QUEEN - Nothing, but that I had not lov'd.

ASTERIA - May I not ask, without offence, who 'tis?

QUEEN - Ev'n that confirms me, I have loved amiss;
Since thou canst know I love, and not imagine
It must be Philocles.

ASTERIA - My cousin is, indeed, a most deserving person;
Valiant, and wise; handsome, and well-born.

QUEEN - But not of royal blood:
I know his fate, unfit to be a king.
To be his wife, I could forsake my crown; but not my glory:
Yet—would he did not love Candiope;
Would he loved me—but knew not of my love,
Or e'er durst tell me his.

ASTERIA - In all this labyrinth,
I find one path, conducting to our quiet.

QUEEN - O tell me quickly then!

ASTERIA - Candiope, as princess of the blood,
Without your approbation cannot marry:
First, break his match with her, by virtue of
Your sovereign authority.

QUEEN - I fear, that were to make him hate me,
Or, what's as bad, to let him know, I love him:
Could you not do it of yourself?

ASTERIA - I'll not be wanting to my pow'r:
But if your majesty appears not in it,
The love of Philocles will soon surmount
All other difficulties.

QUEEN - Then, as we walk, we'll think what means are best;
Effect but this, and thou shar'st half my breast.

[Exeunt.

ACT II
SCENE I—The Queens Apartment

ASTERIA alone.

Nothing thrives that I have plotted;
For I have sounded Philocles, and find
He is too constant to Candiope:
Her too I have assaulted, but in vain,
Objecting want of quality in Philocles.
I'll to the queen, and plainly tell her,
She must make use of her authority
To break the match.

Enter CELADON looking about him.

Brother! what make you here
About the queen's apartments?
Which of the ladies are you watching for?

CELADON - Any of 'em, that will do me the good turn, to make me soundly in love.

ASTERIA - Then I'll bespeak you one, you will be desperately in love with; Florimel: So soon as the queen heard you were returned, she gave you her for mistress.

CELADON - Thank her majesty; but, to confess the truth, my fancy lies partly another way.

ASTERIA - That's strange: Florimel vows you are already in love with her.

CELADON - She wrongs me horribly; if ever I saw or spoke with this Florimel—

ASTERIA - Well, take your fortune, I must leave you.

[Exit ASTERIA.

Enter FLORIMEL, sees him, and is running back.

CELADON - Nay, i'faith I am got betwixt you and home; you are my prisoner, lady bright, till you resolve me one question.

[She makes signs she is dumb.]

Pox, I think, she's dumb: what a vengeance dost thou at court, with such a rare face, without a tongue to answer to a kind question? Art thou dumb indeed? then thou canst tell no tales—

[Goes to kiss her.

FLORIMEL - Hold, hold, you are not mad!

CELADON - Oh, my miss in a mask! have you found your tongue?

FLORIMEL - 'Twas time, I think; what had become of me if I had not?

CELADON - Me thinks your lips had done as well.

FLORIMEL - Ay, if my mask had been over 'em, as it was when you met me in the walks.

CELADON - Well; will you believe me another time? Did not I say, you were infinitely handsome? they may talk of Florimel, if they will, but, i'faith, she must come short of you.

FLORIMEL - Have you seen her, then?

CELADON - I look'd a little that way, but I had soon enough of her; she is not to be seen twice without a surfeit.

FLORIMEL - However, you are beholden to her; they say she loves you.

CELADON - By fate she shan't love me: I have told her a piece of my mind already? Pox o' these coming women: They set a man to dinner, before he has an appetite. [FLAVIA at the door.

FLAVIA - Florimel, you are call'd within—[Exit.

CELADON - I hope in the lord, you are not Florimel!

FLORIMEL - Ev'n she, at your service; the same kind and coming Florimel, you have described.

CELADON - Why then we are agreed already: I am as kind and coming as you, for the heart of you: I knew, at first, we two were good for nothing but one another.

FLORIMEL - But, without raillery, are you in love?

CELADON - So horribly much, that, contrary to my own maxims, I think, in my conscience, I could marry you.

FLORIMEL - No, no, 'tis not come to that yet; but if you are really in love, you have done me the greatest pleasure in the world.

CELADON - That pleasure, and a better too, I have in store for you.

FLORIMEL - This animal, call'd a lover, I have long'd to see these two years.

CELADON - Sure you walk'd with your mask on all the while; for if you had been seen, you could not have been without your wish.

FLORIMEL - I warrant, you mean an ordinary whining lover; but I must have other proofs of love, ere I believe it.

CELADON - You shall have the best that I can give you.

FLORIMEL - I would have a lover, that, if need be, should hang himself, drown himself, break his neck, poison himself, for very despair: He, that will scruple this, is an impudent fellow if he says he is in love.

CELADON - Pray, madam, which of these four things would you have your lover to do? For a man's but a man; he cannot hang, and drown, and break his neck, and poison himself, all together.

FLORIMEL - Well, then, because you are but a beginner, and I would not discourage you, any of these shall serve your turn, in a fair way.

CELADON - I am much deceiv'd in those eyes of yours, if a treat, a song, and the fiddles, be not a more acceptable proof of love to you, than any of those tragical ones you have mentioned.

FLORIMEL - However, you will grant it is but decent you should be pale, and lean, and melancholick, to shew you are in love: And that I shall require of you when I see you next.

CELADON - When you see me next? Why you do not make a rabbit of me, to be lean at twenty-four hours warning? in the mean while, we burn day-light, lose time and love.

FLORIMEL - Would you marry me without consideration?

CELADON - To chuse, by heaven; for they that think on't, twenty to one would never do it. Hang forecast! to make sure of one good night is as much in reason, as a man should expect from this ill world.

FLORIMEL - Methinks, a few more years and discretion would do well: I do not like this going to bed so early; it makes one so weary before morning.

CELADON - That's much as your pillow is laid, before you go to sleep.

FLORIMEL - Shall I make a proposition to you? I will give you a whole year of probation to love me in; to grow reserved, discreet, sober, and faithful, and to pay me all the services of a lover—

CELADON - And at the end of it, you'll marry me?

FLORIMEL - If neither of us alter our minds before.

CELADON - By this light a necessary clause. But if I pay in all the foresaid services before the day, you shall be obliged to take me sooner into mercy.

FLORIMEL - Provided, if you prove unfaithful, then your time of a twelve-month to be prolonged; so many services, I will bate you so many days or weeks; so many faults, I will add to your 'prenticeship so much more: And of all this, I only to be judge.

Enter PHILOCLES and LYSIMANTES.

LYSIMANTES - Is the queen this way, madam?

FLORIMEL - I'll see, so please your highness: Follow me, captive.

CELADON - March on, conqueror—[She pulls him.

[Exeunt CELADON, FLORIMEL.

LYSIMANTES - You're sure her majesty will not oppose it?

PHILOCLES - Leave that to me, my lord.

LYSIMANTES - Then, tho' perhaps my sister's birth might challenge
An higher match,
I'll weigh your merits, on the other side,
To make the balance even.

PHILOCLES - I go, my lord, this minute.

LYSIMANTES - My best wishes wait on you.

[Exit LYSIMANTES.

Enter the QUEEN and ASTERIA.

QUEEN - Yonder he is; have I no other way?

ASTERIA - O madam, you must stand this brunt:
Deny him now, and leave the rest to me:
I'll to Candiope's mother,
And, under the pretence of friendship, work
On her ambition to put off a match
So mean as Philocles.

QUEEN - You may approach, sir; [To PHIL.
We two discourse no secrets.

PHILOCLES - I come, madam, to weary out your royal bounty.

QUEEN - Some suit, I warrant, for your cousin Celadon.
Leave his advancement to my care.

PHILOCLES - Your goodness still prevents my wishes.
Yet I have one request,
Might it not pass almost for madness, and
Extreme ambition in me—

QUEEN - You know you have a favourable judge;
It lies in you not to ask any thing
I cannot grant.

PHILOCLES - Madam, perhaps, you think me too faulty:
But love alone inspires me with ambition,
Tho' but to look on fair Candiope were an excuse for both.

QUEEN - Keep your ambition, and let love alone:
That I can cloy, but this I cannot cure.
I have some reasons (invincible to me) which must forbid
Your marriage with Candiope.

PHILOCLES - I knew I was not worthy.

QUEEN - Not for that, Philocles; you deserve all things,
And, to shew I think it, my admiral, I hear, is dead;
His vacant place (the best in all my kingdom,)
I here confer on you.

PHILOCLES - Rather take back all you had giv'n before,
Than not give this;
For believe, madam, nothing is so near
My soul, as the possession of Candiope.

QUEEN - Since that belief would be to your disadvantage,
I will not entertain it.

PHILOCLES - Why, madam, can you be thus cruel to me?
To give me all things, which I did not ask,
And yet deny that only thing, I beg:
And so beg, that I find I cannot live
Without the hope of it.

QUEEN - Hope greater things;
But hope not this. Haste to o'ercome your love;
It is but putting a short-liv'd passion to a violent death.

PHILOCLES - I cannot live without Candiope;
But I can die, without a murmur,
Having my doom pronounced from your fair mouth.

QUEEN - If I am to pronounce it, live, my Philocles,
But live without, (I was about to say) [Aside.
Without his love, but that I cannot do;

Live Philocles without Candiope.

PHILOCLES - Madam, could you give my doom so quickly,
And knew it was irrevocable!
'Tis too apparent,
You, who alone love glory, and whose soul
Is loosened from your senses, cannot judge
What torments mine, of grosser mould, endures.

QUEEN - I cannot suffer you
To give me praises, which are not my own:
I love like you, and am yet much more wretched,
Than you can think yourself.

PHILOCLES - Weak bars they needs must be, that fortune puts
'Twixt sovereign power, and all it can desire.
When princes love, they call themselves unhappy;
Only, because the word sounds handsome in a lover's mouth;
But you can cease to be so when you please,
By making Lysimantes fortunate.

QUEEN - Were he indeed the man, you had some reason;
But 'tis another, more without my power,
And yet a subject too.

PHILOCLES - O, madam, say not so:
It cannot be a subject, if not he;
It were to be injurious to yourself
To make another choice.

QUEEN - Yet, Lysimantes, set by him I love,
Is more obscured, than stars too near the sun:
He has a brightness of his own,
Not borrowed of his father's, but born with him.

PHILOCLES - Pardon me if I say, whoe'er he be,
He has practis'd some ill arts upon you, madam;
For he, whom you describe, I see, is born
But from the lees o' the people.

QUEEN - You offend me, Philocles.
Whence had you leave to use those insolent terms,
Of him I please to love? One, I must tell you,
(Since foolishly I have gone thus far)
Whom I esteem your equal,
And far superior to prince Lysimantes;
One, who deserves to wear a crown—

PHILOCLES - Whirlwinds bear me hence, before I live
To that detested day!—That frown assures me
I have offended, by my over-freedom;

But yet, methinks, a heart so plain and honest,
And zealous of your glory, might hope your pardon for it.

QUEEN - I give it you; but,
When you know him better,
You'll alter your opinion; he's no ill friend of yours.

PHILOCLES - I well perceive,
He has supplanted me in your esteem;
But that's the least of ills this fatal wretch
Has practised—Think, for heaven's sake, madam, think,
If you have drunk no philtre.

QUEEN - Yes, he has given me a philtre;
But I have drunk it only from his eyes.

PHILOCLES - Hot irons thank 'em for't!
[Softly, or turning from her.

QUEEN - What's that you mutter?
Hence from my sight! I know not whether
I ever shall endure to see you more.

PHILOCLES - But hear me, madam.

QUEEN - I say, begone. See me no more this day.
I will not hear one word in your excuse:
Now, sir, be rude again; and give laws to your queen.

[Exit PHILOCLES bowing.

Asteria, come hither.
Was ever boldness like to this of Philocles?
Help me to reproach him, for I resolve
Henceforth no more to love him.

ASTERIA - Truth is, I wondered at your patience, madam:
Did you not mark his words, his mein, his action,
How full of haughtiness, how small respect?

QUEEN - And he to use me thus, he whom I favoured,
Nay more, he whom I loved?

ASTERIA - A man, methinks, of vulgar parts and presence!

QUEEN - Or, allow him something handsome, valiant,
Or so—Yet this to me!—

ASTERIA - The workmanship of inconsiderate favour,
The creature of rash love; one of those meteors
Which monarchs raise from earth,

And people, wondering how they came so high,
Fear, from their influence, plagues, and wars, and famine.

QUEEN - Ha!

ASTERIA - One, whom, instead of banishing a day,
You should have plumed of all his borrowed honours,
And let him see what abject things they are,
Whom princes often love without desert.

QUEEN - What has my Philocles deserved from thee,
That thou shouldst use him thus?
Were he the basest of mankind, thou couldst not
Have given him ruder language.

ASTERIA - Did not your majesty command me?
Did not yourself begin?

QUEEN - I grant I did, but I have right to do it:
I love him, and may rail; in you 'tis malice;
Malice in the most high degree; for never man
Was more deserving than my Philocles.
Or, do you love him, ha! and plead that title?
Confess, and I'll forgive you—
For none can look on him, but needs must love.

ASTERIA - I love him, madam! I beseech your majesty,
Have better thoughts of me.

QUEEN - Dost thou not love him then?
Good heaven, how stupid, and how dull is she?
How most invincibly insensible!
No woman does deserve to live,
That loves not Philocles.

ASTERIA - Dear madam, recollect yourself; alas!
How much distracted are your thoughts; and how
Disjointed all your words!
The sibyl's leaves more orderly were laid.
Where is that harmony of mind, that prudence,
Which guided all you did? that sense of glory,
Which raised you high above the rest of kings,
As kings are o'er the level of mankind?

QUEEN - Gone, gone, Asteria; all is gone,
Or lost within me, far from any use.
Sometimes I struggle, like the sun in clouds,
But straight I am o'ercast.

ASTERIA - I grieve to see it.

QUEEN - Then thou hast yet the goodness
To pardon what I said?
Alas! I use myself much worse than thee.
Love rages in great souls,
For there his power most opposition finds;
High trees are shook, because they dare the winds.

[Exeunt.

Act III

SCENE I—The Court Gallery.

PHILOCLES solus.

'Tis true, she banished me but for a day;
But favourites, once declining, sink apace.
Yet fortune, stop—this is the likeliest place
To meet Asteria, and by her convey
My humble vows to my offended queen.
Ha! She comes herself; unhappy man,
Where shall I hide?—[Is going out.

Enter QUEEN and ASTERIA.

QUEEN - Is not that Philocles,
Who makes such haste away? Philocles, Philocles!—

PHILOCLES - I feared she saw me. [Coming back.

QUEEN - How now, sir, am I such a bugbear,
That I scare people from me?

PHILOCLES - 'Tis true, I should more carefully have shunned
The place where you might be; as, when it thunders,
Men reverently quit the open air,
Because the angry gods are then abroad.

QUEEN - What does he mean, Asteria?
I do not understand him.

ASTERIA - Your majesty forgets, you banished him
Your presence for this day. [To her softly.

QUEEN - Ha! banished him! 'tis true indeed;
But, as thou sayest, I had forgot it quite.

ASTERIA - That's very strange, scarce half an hour ago.

QUEEN - But love had drawn his pardon up so soon,
That I forgot he e'er offended me.

PHILOCLES - Pardon me, that I could not thank you sooner;
Your sudden grace, like some swift flood poured in
On narrow banks, o'erflowed my spirits.

QUEEN - No: 'tis for me to ask your pardon, Philocles,
For the great injury I did you,
In not remembering I was angry with you:
But I'll repair my fault,
And rouse my anger up against you yet.

PHILOCLES - No, madam, my forgiveness was your act of grace,
And I lay hold of it.

QUEEN - Princes sometimes may pass
Acts of oblivion, in their own wrong.

PHILOCLES - 'Tis true, but not recal them.

QUEEN - But, Philocles, since I have told you there is one
I love, I will go on, and let you know
What passed this day betwixt us; be our judge,
Whether my servant have dealt well with me.

PHILOCLES - I beseech your majesty, excuse me:
Any thing more of him may make me
Relapse too soon, and forfeit my late pardon.

QUEEN - But you'll be glad to know it.

PHILOCLES - May I not hope, then,
You have some quarrel to him?

QUEEN - Yes, a great one.
But first to justify myself:
Know, Philocles, I have concealed my passion
With such care from him, that he knows not yet
I love, but only that I much esteem him.

PHILOCLES - O stupid wretch,
That, by a thousand tokens, could not guess it!

QUEEN - He loves elsewhere, and that has blinded him.

PHILOCLES - He's blind indeed!
So the dull beasts in the first paradise,
With levelled eyes, gazed each upon their kind;
There fixed their love, and ne'er looked up to view
That glorious creature man, their sovereign lord.

QUEEN - Y'are too severe on little faults; but he
Has crimes, untold,
Which will, I fear, move you much more against him.
He fell this day into a passion with me,
And boldly contradicted all I said.

PHILOCLES - And stands his head upon his shoulders yet?
How long shall this most insolent—

QUEEN - Take heed you rail not;
You know you are but on your good behaviour.

PHILOCLES - Why then I will not call him traitor,
But only rude, audacious, and impertinent,
To use his sovereign so—I beg your leave
To wish, you have at least imprisoned him.

QUEEN - Some people may speak ill, and yet mean well:
Remember you were not confined; and yet
Your fault was great. In short, I love him,
And that excuses all; but be not jealous;
His rising shall not be your overthrow,
Nor will I ever marry him.

PHILOCLES - That's some comfort yet;
He shall not be a king.

QUEEN - He never shall. But you are discomposed;
Stay here a little; I have somewhat for you,
Shall shew, you still are in my favour.

[Exeunt QUEEN and ASTERIA.

Enter to him CANDIOPE, weeping.

PHILOCLES - How now, in tears, my fair Candiope?
So, through a watry cloud,
The sun, at once, seems both to weep and shine.
For what forefather's sin do you afflict
Those precious eyes? For sure you have
None of your own to weep.

CANDIOPE - My crimes both great and many needs must shew,
Since heaven will punish them with losing you.

PHILOCLES - Afflictions, sent from heaven without a cause,
Make bold mankind enquire into its laws.
But heaven, which moulding beauty takes such care,
Makes gentle fates on purpose for the fair:
And destiny, that sees them so divine,

Spins all their fortunes in a silken twine:
No mortal hand so ignorant is found,
To weave coarse work upon a precious ground.

CANDIOPE - Go preach this doctrine in my mother's ears.

PHILOCLES - Has her severity produced these tears?

CANDIOPE - She has recalled those hopes she gave before,
And strictly bids me ne'er to see you more.

PHILOCLES - Changes in froward age are natural;
Who hopes for constant weather in the fall?
'Tis in your power your duty to transfer,
And place that right in me, which was in her.

CANDIOPE - Reason, like foreign foes, would ne'er o'ercome,
But that I find I am betrayed at home;
You have a friend, that fights for you within.

PHILOCLES - Let reason ever lose, so love may win.

Enter QUEEN with a picture in her hand, and ASTERIA

QUEEN - See there, Asteria,
All we have done succeeds still to the worse;
We hindered him from seeing her at home,
Where I but only heard they loved; and now
She comes to court, and mads me with the sight on't.
ASTERIA - Dear madam, overcome yourself a little,
Or they'll perceive how much you are concerned.

QUEEN - I struggle with my heart—
But it will have some vent.
Cousin, you are a stranger at the court. [To CANDIOPE.

CANDIOPE - It was my duty, I confess,
To attend oftner on your majesty.

QUEEN - Asteria, mend my cousin's handkerchief;
It sits too narrow there, and shows too much
The broadness of her shoulders—Nay, fie, Asteria,
Now you put it too much backward, and discover
The bigness of her breasts.

CANDIOPE - I beseech your majesty,
Give not yourself this trouble.

QUEEN - Sweet cousin, you shall pardon me;
A beauty such as yours
Deserves a more than ordinary care,

To set it out.
Come hither, Philocles, do but observe,
She has but one gross fault in all her shape,
That is, she bears up here too much,
And the malicious workman has left it
Open to your eye.

PHILOCLES - Where, and please your majesty?
Methinks 'tis very well.

QUEEN - Do not you see it? Oh how blind is love!

CANDIOPE - And how quick-sighted malice! [Aside.

QUEEN - But yet, methinks, those knots of sky do not
So well with the dead colour of her face.

ASTERIA - Your majesty mistakes, she wants no red.

[The QUEEN here plucks out her glass, and looks sometimes on herself, sometimes on her rival.

QUEEN - How do I look to-day, Asteria?
Methinks, not well.

ASTERIA - Pardon me, madam, most victoriously.

QUEEN - What think you, Philocles? come, do not flatter.

PHILOCLES - Paris was a bold man, who presumed,
To judge the beauty of a goddess.

CANDIOPE - Your majesty has given the reason why
He cannot judge; his love has blinded him.

QUEEN - Methinks, a long patch here, beneath her eye,
Might hide that dismal hollowness.
What think you, Philocles?

CANDIOPE - Beseech you, madam, ask not his opinion:
What my faults are it is no matter;
He loves me with them all.

QUEEN - Ay, he may love; but when he marries you,
Your bridal shall be kept in some dark dungeon.
Farewell, and think of that, too easy maid!
I blush, thou sharest my blood.

[Exeunt QUEEN and ASTERIA.

CANDIOPE - Inhuman queen!
Thou canst not be more willing to resign

Thy part in me, than I to give up mine.

PHILOCLES - Love, how few subjects do thy laws fulfil,
And yet those few, like us, thou usest ill!

CANDIOPE - The greatest slaves, in monarchies, are they,
Whom birth sets nearest to imperial sway;
While jealous power does sullenly o'erspy,
We play, like deer, within the lion's eye.
'Would I for you some shepherdess had been,
And, but each May, ne'er heard the name of queen!

PHILOCLES - If you were so, might I some monarch be,
Then, you should gain what now you lose by me;
Then, you in all my glories should have part,
And rule my empire, as you rule my heart.

CANDIOPE - How much our golden wishes are in vain!
When they are past, we are ourselves again.

Enter QUEEN and ASTERIA above.

QUEEN - Look, look, Asteria, yet they are not gone.
Hence we may hear what they discourse alone.

PHILOCLES - My love inspires me with a generous thought,
Which you, unknowing in those wishes, taught.
Since happiness may out of courts be found,
Why stay we here on this enchanted ground;
And chuse not rather with content to dwell
(If love and joy can find it) in a cell?

CANDIOPE - Those who, like you, have once in courts been great,
May think they wish, but wish not, to retreat.
They seldom go, but when they cannot stay;
As losing gamesters throw the dice away.
Even in that cell, where you repose would find,
Visions of court will haunt your restless mind;
And glorious dreams stand ready to restore
The pleasing shapes of all you had before.

PHILOCLES - He, who with your possession once is blest,
On easy terms will part with all the rest.
All my ambition will in you be crowned;
And those white arms shall all my wishes bound.
Our life shall be but one long nuptial day,
And, like chafed odours, melt in sweets away;
Soft as the night our minutes shall be worn,
And chearful as the birds, that wake the morn.

CANDIOPE - Thus hope misleads itself in pleasant way,

And takes more joys on trust, than love can pay:
But, love with long possession once decayed,
That face, which now you court, you will upbraid.

PHILOCLES - False lovers broach these tenets, to remove
The fault from them, by placing it on love.

CANDIOPE - Yet grant, in youth you keep alive your fire,
Old age will come, and then it must expire:
Youth but a while does at love's temple stay,
As some fair inn, to lodge it on the way.

PHILOCLES - Your doubts are kind; but, to be satisfied
I can be true, I beg I may be tried.

CANDIOPE - Trials of love too dear the making cost;
For if successless, the whole venture's lost.
What you propose, brings wants and care along.

PHILOCLES - Love can bear both.

CANDIOPE - But is your love so strong?

PHILOCLES - They do not want, who wish not to have more;
Who ever said an anchoret was poor?

CANDIOPE - To answer generously, as you have done,
I should not by your arguments be won:
I know, I urge your ruin by consent;
Yet love too well, that ruin to prevent.

PHILOCLES - Like water given to those whom fevers fry,
You kill but him, who must without it die.

CANDIOPE - Secure me, I may love without a crime;
Then, for our flight, appoint both place and time.

PHILOCLES - The ensuing hour my plighted vows shall be;
The time's not long; or only long to me.

CANDIOPE - Then, let us go where we shall ne'er be seen
By my hard mother.

PHILOCLES - Or my cruel queen.

[Exeunt PHILOCLES and CANDIOPE.

QUEEN [above] - O, Philocles, unkind to call me cruel!
So false Aeneas did from Dido fly;
But never branded her with cruelty.
How I despise myself for loving so!

ASTERIA - At once you hate yourself, and love him too.

QUEEN - No, his ingratitude has cured my wound:
A painful cure indeed!

ASTERIA - And yet not sound.
His ignorance of your true thoughts
Excuses this; you did seem cruel, madam.

QUEEN - But much of kindness still mixed with it.
Who could mistake so grossly, not to know
A Cupid frowning, when he draws his bow?

ASTERIA - He's going now to smart for his offence.

QUEEN - Should he, without my leave, depart from hence?

ASTERIA - No matter; since you hate him, let him go.

QUEEN - But I my hate by my revenge will show:
Besides, his head's a forfeit to the state.

ASTERIA - When you take that, I will believe you hate.
Let him possess, and then he'll soon repent;
And so his crime will prove his punishment.

QUEEN - He may repent; but he will first possess.

ASTERIA - O, madam, now your hatred you confess:
If his possessing her your rage does move,
'Tis jealousy, the avarice of love.

QUEEN - No more, Asteria.
Seek Lysimantes out, bid him set his guards
Through all the court and city.
Prevent their marriage first; then stop their flight.
Some fitting punishments I will ordain,
But speak not you of Philocles again:
'Tis bold to search, and dangerous to find,
Too much of heaven's, or of a prince's mind.

[QUEEN descends, and exit.

As the QUEEN has done speaking, FLAVIA is going hastily over the stage; ASTERIA sees her.

ASTERIA - Flavia, Flavia, whither so fast?

FLAVIA - Did you call, Asteria?

ASTERIA - The queen has business with Prince Lysimantes;

Speak to any gentleman in the court, to fetch him.

[Exit ASTERIA from above.

FLAVIA - I suspect somewhat, but I'll watch you close;
Prince Lysimantes has not chose in me
The worst spy of the court—
Celadon! what makes he here?

Enter CELADON, OLINDA, and SABINA; they walk over the stage together, he seeming to court them.

OLINDA - Nay, sweet Celadon—

SABRINA - Nay, dear Celadon.

FLAVIA - O ho! I see his business now; 'tis with Melissa's two daughters: Look, look, how he peeps about, to see if the coast be clear; like an hawk that will not plume, if she be looked on.

[Exeunt CELADON, OLINDA and SABINA.

So—at last he has trussed his quarry.

Enter FLORIMEL.

FLORIMEL - Did you see Celadon this way?

FLAVIA - If you had not asked the question, I should have thought you had come from watching him; he's just gone off with Melissa's daughters.

FLORIMEL - Melissa's daughters! he did not court 'em, I hope?

FLAVIA - So busily, he lost no time: While he was teaching the one a tune, he was kissing the other's hand.

FLORIMEL - O fine gentleman!

FLAVIA - And they so greedy of him! did you never see two fishes about a bait, tugging it this way and t'other way? for my part, I looked at least he should have lost a leg or arm i'the service. Nay, never vex yourself, but e'en resolve to break with him.

FLORIMEL - No, no, 'tis not come to that yet; I'll correct him first, and then hope the best from time.

FLAVIA - From time! believe me, there's little good to be expected from him. I never knew the old gentleman with the scythe and hour-glass bring any thing but grey hair, thin cheeks, and loss of teeth: You see Celadon loves others.

FLORIMEL - There's the more hope he may love me among the rest: Hang it, I would not marry one of these solemn fops; they are good for nothing, but to make cuckolds. Give me a servant, that is an high flier at all games, that is bounteous of himself to many women; and yet, whenever I pleased to throw out the lure of matrimony, should come down with a swing, and fly the better at his own quarry.

FLAVIA - But are you sure you can take him down when you think good?

FLORIMEL - Nothing more certain.

FLAVIA - What wager will you venture upon the trial?

FLORIMEL - Any thing.

FLAVIA - My maidenhead to yours.

FLORIMEL - That's a good one; who shall take the forfeit?

FLAVIA - I'll go and write a letter, as from these two sisters, to summon him immediately; it shall be delivered before you. I warrant, you see a strange combat betwixt the flesh and the spirit: If he leaves you to go to them, you'll grant he loves them better?

FLORIMEL - Not a jot the more: A bee may pick of many flowers, and yet like some one better than all the rest.

FLAVIA - But then your bee must not leave his sting behind him.

FLORIMEL - Well; make the experiment however: I hear him coming, and a whole noise of fidlers at his heels. Hey-day, what a mad husband shall I have!—

Enter CELADON.

FLAVIA - And what a mad wife will he have! Well, I must go a little way, but I'll return immediately, and write it: You'll keep him in discourse the while? [Exit FLA.

CELADON - Where are you, madam? What, do you mean to run away thus? Pray stand to't, that we may despatch this business.

FLORIMEL - I think you mean to watch me, as they do witches, to make me confess I love you. Lord, what a bustle have you kept this afternoon? What with eating, singing, and dancing, I am so wearied, that I shall not be in case to hear any more love this fortnight.

CELADON - Nay, if you surfeit on't before trial, Lord have mercy upon you, when I have married you.

FLORIMEL - But what king's revenue, do you think, will maintain this extravagant expence?

CELADON - I have a damnable father, a rich old rogue, if he would once die! Lord, how long does he mean to make it ere he dies!

FLORIMEL - As long as ever he can, I'll pass my word for him.

CELADON - I think, then, we had best consider him as an obstinate old fellow, that is deaf to the news of a better world; and ne'er stay for him.

FLORIMEL - But e'en marry; and get him grandchildren in abundance, and great-grandchildren upon them, and so inch him and shove him out of the world by the very force of new generations—if that be the way, you must excuse me.

CELADON - But dost thou know what it is to be an old maid?

FLORIMEL - No, nor hope I shan't these twenty years.

CELADON - But when that time comes, in the first place, thou wilt be condemned to tell stories, how many men thou mightst have had; and none believe thee: Then thou growest forward, and impudently weariest all thy friends to solicit man for thee.

FLORIMEL - Away with your old common-place-wit: I am resolved to grow fat, and look young till forty, and then slip out of the world, with the first wrinkle, and the reputation of five and twenty.

CELADON - Well, what think you now of a reckoning betwixt us?

FLORIMEL - How do you mean?

CELADON - To discount for so many days of my years service, as I have paid in this morning.

FLORIMEL - With all my heart.

CELADON - Imprimis, for a treat.
Item, For my glass coach.
Item, For sitting bare, and wagging your fan.
And lastly, and principally, for my fidelity to you this long hour and half.

FLORIMEL - For this I bate you three weeks of your service; now hear your bill of faults; for your comfort 'tis a short one.

CELADON - I know it.

FLORIMEL - Imprimis, item, and sum total, for keeping company with Melissa's daughters.

CELADON - How the pox came you to know of that? Gad, I believe the devil plays booty against himself, and tells you of my sins. [Aside.

FLORIMEL - The offence being so small, the punishment shall be but proportionable; I will set you back only half a year.

CELADON - You're most unconscionable: When then do you think we shall come together? There's none but the old patriarchs could live long enough to marry you at this rate. What, do you take me for some cousin of Methusalem's, that I must stay an hundred years, before I come to beget sons and daughters?

FLORIMEL - Here's an impudent lover! he complains of me without ever offering to excuse himself; item, a fortnight more for that.

CELADON - So, there's another puff in my voyage, has blown me back to the north of Scotland.

FLORIMEL - All this is nothing to your excuse for the two sisters.

CELADON - 'Faith, if ever I did more than kiss them, and that but once—

FLORIMEL - What could you have done more to me?

CELADON - An hundred times more; as thou shalt know, dear rogue, at time convenient.

FLORIMEL - You talk, you talk; could you kiss them, though but once, and ne'er think of me?

CELADON - Nay, if I had thought of thee, I had kissed them over a thousand times, with the very force of imagination.

FLORIMEL - The gallants are mightily beholden to you; you have found them out a new way to kiss their mistresses, upon other women's lips.

CELADON - What would you have? You are my Sultana Queen, the rest are but in the nature of your slaves; I may make some slight excursions into the enemy's country for forage, or so, but I ever return to my head quarters.

Enter one with a letter.

CELADON - To me?

MESSENGER - If your name be Celadon. [CELADON - reads softly.

FLORIMEL - He is swallowing the pill; presently we shall see the operation.

CELADON - to the page.] Child, come hither, child; here's money for thee: So, begone quickly, good child, before any body examines thee: Thou art in a dangerous place, child—[Thrusts him out.] Very good; the sisters send me word, they will have the fiddles this afternoon, and invite me to sup there!—Now, cannot I forbear, an I should be damned, tho' I have scap'd a scouring so lately for it. Yet I love Florimel better than both of them together; there's the riddle on't: But only for the sweet sake of variety. [Aside.] Well, we must all sin, and we must all repent, and there's an end on't.

FLORIMEL - What is it, that makes you fidge up and down so?

CELADON - 'Faith, I am sent for by a very dear friend, and 'tis upon a business of life and death.

FLORIMEL - On my life, some woman?

CELADON - On my honour, some man; do you think I would lie to you?

FLORIMEL - But you engaged to sup with me.

CELADON - But I consider it may be scandalous to stay late in your lodgings. Adieu, dear miss! If ever I am false to thee again!—

[Exit CELADON.

FLORIMEL - See what constant metal you men are made of! He begins to vex me in good earnest. Hang him, let him go and take enough of 'em: And yet, methinks, I can't endure he should neither. Lord, that such a mad-cap as I should ever live to be jealous! I must after him.
Some ladies would discard him now, but I
A fitter way for my revenge will find;
I'll marry him, and serve him in his kind.

[Exit FLORIMEL.

ACT IV

SCENE I—The Walks

MELISSA, after her OLINDA and SABINA.

MELISSA - I must take this business up in time: This wild fellow begins to haunt my house again. Well, I'll be bold to say it, 'tis as easy to bring up a young lion without mischief, as a maidenhead of fifteen, to make it tame for an husband's bed. Not but that the young man is handsome, rich, and young, and I could be content he should marry one of them; but to seduce them both in this manner:—Well, I'll examine them apart, and if I can find out which he loves, I'll offer him his choice. Olinda, come hither, child.

OLINDA - Your pleasure, madam?

MELISSA - Nothing but for your good, Olinda; what think you of Celadon?

OLINDA - Why I think he's a very mad fellow; but yet I have some obligements to him: he teaches me new airs of the guitar, and talks wildly to me, and I to him.

MELISSA - But tell me in earnest, do you think he loves you?

OLINDA - Can you doubt it? There were never two so cut out for one another; we both love singing, dancing, treats, and music. In short, we are each other's counterpart.

MELISSA - But does he love you seriously?

OLINDA - Seriously?—I know not that; if he did, perhaps I should not love him: But we sit and talk, and wrangle, and are friends; when we are together, we never hold our tongues; and then we have always a noise of fiddles at our heels; he hunts me merrily, as the hound does the hare; and either this is love, or I know it not.

MELISSA - Well, go back, and call Sabina to me.

[OLINDA goes behind.

This is a riddle past my finding out: Whether he loves her, or no, is the question; but this, I am sure of, she loves him:—O my little favourite, I must ask you a question concerning Celadon: is he in love with you?

SABRINA - I think, indeed, he does not hate me; at least, if a man's word may be taken for it.

MELISSA - But what expressions has he made you?

SABRINA - Truly, the man has done his part: He has spoken civilly to me, and I was not so young but I understood him.

MELISSA - And you could be content to marry him?

SABRINA - I have sworn never to marry: besides he's a wild young man; yet, to obey you, mother, I would be content to be sacrificed.

MELISSA - No, no, we would but lead you to the altar.

SABRINA - Not to put off the gentleman neither; for if I have him not, I am resolved to die a maid, that's once, mother.

MELISSA - Both my daughters are in love with him, and I cannot yet find he loves either of them.

OLINDA - Mother, mother, yonder's Celadon in the walks.

MELISSA - Peace, wanton; you had best ring the bells for joy. Well, I'll not meet him, because I know not which to offer him; yet he seems to like the youngest best: I'll give him opportunity with her. Olinda, do you make haste after me.

OLINDA - This is something hard though.

[Exit MELISSA.

Enter CELADON.

CELADON - You see, ladies, the least breath of yours brings me to you: I have been seeking you at your lodgings, and from thence came hither after you.

SABRINA - 'Twas well you found us.

CELADON - Found you! half this brightness betwixt you two was enough to have lighted me; I could never miss my way: Here's fair Olinda has beauty enough for one family; such a voice, such a wit, so noble a stature, so white a skin!—

OLINDA - I thought he would be particular at last [Aside.

CELADON - And young Sabina, so sweet an innocence, such a rose-bud newly blown. This is my goodly palace of love, and that my little withdrawing room. A word, madam. [To SABINA.

OLINDA - I like not this—[Aside.] Sir, if you are not too busy with my sister, I would speak with you.

CELADON - I come, madam.

SABRINA - Time enough, sir; pray finish your discourse—and as you were a saying, sir,—

OLINDA - Sweet sir,—

SABRINA - Sister, you forget, my mother bid you make haste.

OLINDA - Well, go you, and tell her I am coming.

SABRINA - I can never endure to be the messenger of ill news; but, if you please, I'll send her word you won't come.

OLINDA - Minion, minion, remember this—[Exit OLIN.

SABRINA - She's horribly in love with you.

CELADON - Lord, who could love that walking steeple! She's so high, that every time she sings to me, I am looking up for the bell that tolls to church. Ha! give me my little fifth-rate, that lies so snug. She! hang her, a Dutch-built bottom: She's so tall, there's no boarding her. But we lose time—madam, let me seal my love upon your mouth. [Kiss] Soft and sweet, by heaven! sure you wear rose-leaves between your lips.

SABRINA - Lord, Lord, what's the matter with me! my breath grows so short, I can scarce speak to you.

CELADON - No matter, give me thy lips again, and I'll speak for thee.

SABRINA - You don't love me—

CELADON - I warrant thee; sit down by me, and kiss again,—She warms faster than Pygmalion's image. [Aside]—[Kiss.]—Ay marry, sir, this was the original use of lips; talking, eating, and drinking came in by and by.

SABRINA - Nay, pray be civil; will you be at quiet?

CELADON - What, would you have me sit still, and look upon you, like a little puppy-dog, that's taught to beg with his fore-leg up?

Enter FLORIMEL.

FLORIMEL - Celadon the faithful! in good time, sir,—

CELADON - In very good time, Florimel; for heaven's sake, help me quickly.

FLORIMEL - What's the matter?

CELADON - Do you not see? here's a poor gentlewoman in a swoon! (Swoon away.) I have been rubbing her this half hour, and cannot bring her to her senses.

FLORIMEL - Alas! how came she so?

CELADON - Oh barbarous! do you stay to ask questions? run, for charity.

FLORIMEL - Help, help! alas! poor lady—[Exit FLORIMEL.

SABRINA - Is she gone?

CELADON - Ay, thanks be to my wit, that helped me at a pinch; I thank heaven, I never pumpt for a lye in all my life yet.

SABRINA - I am afraid you love her, Celadon!

CELADON - Only as a civil acquaintance, or so; but, however, to avoid slander, you had best be gone before she comes again.

SABRINA - I can find a tongue as well as she.

CELADON - Ay, but the truth is, I am a kind of scandalous person, and for you to be seen in my company—stay in the walks, by this kiss I'll be with you presently.

Enter FLORIMEL running.

FLORIMEL - Help, help!—I can find nobody.

CELADON - Tis needless now, my dear; she's recovered, and gone off; but so wan and weakly,—

FLORIMEL - Umph! I begin to smell a rat. What was your business here, Celadon?

CELADON - Charity, Christian charity; you saw I was labouring for life with her.

FLORIMEL - But how came you hither?—Not that I care this, but only to be satisfied. [Sings.

CELADON - You are jealous, in my conscience!

FLORIMEL - Who, I jealous!—then I wish this sigh may be the last that ever I may draw. [Sighs.

CELADON - But why do you sigh, then?

FLORIMEL - Nothing but a cold, I cannot fetch my breath well. But what will you say, if I wrote the letter you had, to try your faith?

CELADON - Hey day! this is just the devil and the sinner; you lay snares for me, and then punish me for being taken: Here's trying a man's faith indeed!—What, do you think I had the faith of a stock, or of a stone? Nay, an you go to tantalize a man—I love upon the square, I can endure no tricks to be used to me.

[OLINDA and SABINA at the door peeping.

OLINDA - and SABRINA - Celadon! Celadon!

FLORIMEL - What voices are those?

CELADON - Some comrades of mine, that call me to play. Pox on them, they'll spoil all. [Aside.

FLORIMEL - Pray, let's see them.

CELADON - Hang them, tatterdemallions! they are not worth your sight. Pray, gentlemen, begone; I'll be with you immediately.

SABRINA - No; we'll stay here for you.

FLORIMEL - Do your gentlemen speak with treble voices? I am resolved to see what company you keep.

CELADON - Nay, good my dear.

[He lays hold of her to pull her back, she lays hold of OLINDA, by whom SABRINA holds; so that, he pulling, they all come in.

FLORIMEL - Are these your comrades? [Sings.] 'Tis Strephon calls, what would my love? Why do you not roar out, like a great bass-viol, Come follow to the myrtle-grove. Pray, sir, which of these fair ladies is it, for whom you were to do the courtesy? for it were unconscionable to leave you to them both:—What, a mans but a man, you know.

OLINDA - The gentleman may find an owner.

SABRINA - Though not of you.

FLORIMEL - Pray, agree whose the lost sheep is, and take him.

CELADON - 'Slife, they'll cry me anon, and tell my marks.

FLORIMEL - Troth, I pity your highness there; I perceive he has left you for the little one: Methinks he should have been afraid to break his neck, when he fell so high as from you to her.

SABRINA - Well, my drolling lady, I may be even with you.

FLORIMEL - Not this ten years, by the growth, yet.

SABRINA - Can flesh and blood endure this!

FLORIMEL - How now, my amazon in decimo sexto!

OLINDA - Do you affront my sister?

FLORIMEL - Ay; but thou art so tall, I think I shall never affront thee.

SABRINA - Come away, sister; we shall be jeered to death else. [Exeunt OLINDA - and SAB.

FLORIMEL - Why do you look that way? You can't forbear leering after the forbidden fruit. But whene'er I take a wencher's word again!

CELADON - A wencher's word!—Why should you speak so contemptibly of the better half of mankind? I'll stand up for the honour of my vocation.

FLORIMEL - You are in no fault, I warrant!—'Ware my busk[A].

[Footnote A: The now almost forgotten busk was a small slip of steel or wood, used to stiffen the stays. Florimel threatens to employ it as a rod of chastisement.]

CELADON - Not to give a fair lady the lie, I am in fault; but otherwise—Come, let us be friends, and let me wait on you to your lodgings.

FLORIMEL - This impudence shall not save you from my table-book. Item, A month more for this fault. [They walk to the door.

1ST SOLDIER - [within.] Stand!—

2ND SOLDIER - Stand, give the word!

CELADON - Now, what's the meaning of this, trow?—guards set!

1ST SOLDIER - Give the word, or you cannot pass:—These are they, brother; let's in and seize them.

The two Soldiers enter.

1ST SOLDIER - Down with him!

2ND SOLDIER - Disarm him!

CELADON - How now, rascals?— [Draws, and beats one off, and catches the other. Ask your life, you villain.

2ND SOLDIER - Quarter! quarter!

CELADON - Was ever such an insolence?

2ND SOLDIER - We did but our duty;—here we were set to take a gentleman and lady, that would steal a marriage without the queen's consent, and we thought you had been they. [Exit Sold.

FLORIMEL - Your cousin Philocles, and the princess Candiope, on my life! for I heard the queen give private orders to Lysimantes, and name them twice or thrice.

CELADON - I know a score or two of madcaps here hard by, whom I can pick up from taverns, and gaming-houses, and bordels; those I'll bring to aid him,—Now, Florimel, there's an argument for wenching: Where would you have had so many honest men together, upon the sudden, for a brave employment?

FLORIMEL - You'll leave me then, to take my fortune?

CELADON - No:—If you will, I'll have you into the places aforesaid, and enter you into good company.

FLORIMEL - 'Thank you, sir; here's a key, will let me through this back-door to my own lodgings.

CELADON - If I come off with life, I'll see you this evening; if not,—adieu, Florimel!

FLORIMEL - If you come not, I shall conclude you are killed; or taken, to be hanged for a rebel to-morrow morning: and then I'll honour your memory with a lampoon, instead of an epitaph.

CELADON - No, no! I trust better in my fate: I know I am reserved to do you a courtesy. [Exit CEL.

[As FLORIMEL is unlocking the door to go out, FLAVIA opens it against her, and enters to her, followed by a Page.

FLAVIA - Florimel, do you hear the news?

FLORIMEL - I guess they are in pursuit of Philocles.

FLAVIA - When Lysimantes came with the queen's orders,
He refused to render up Candìope;
And, with some few brave friends he had about him,
Is forcing of his way through all the guards.

FLORIMEL - A gallant fellow!—I'll in, will you with me?— Hark! the noise comes this way!

FLAVIA - I have a message from the queen to Lysimantes. I hope I may be safe among the soldiers.

FLORIMEL - Oh, very safe!—Perhaps some honest fellow in the tumult may take pity of thy maidenhead, or so. Adieu!

[Exit FLORIMEL.

PAGE - The noise comes nearer, madam.

FLAVIA - I am glad on't. This message gives me the opportunity of speaking privately with Lysimantes.

Enter PHILOCLES and CANDIOPE, with three Friends, pursued by LYSIMANTES, and Soldiers.

LYSIMANTES - What is it renders you thus obstinate? You have no hope of flight, and to resist is full as vain.

PHILOCLES - I'll die rather than yield her up.

FLAVIA - My lord!

LYSIMANTES - How now? some new message from the queen?— Retire a while to a convenient distance.

[To the Soldiers. LYSIMANTES and FLAVIA whisper.

LYSIMANTES - O Flavia, 'tis impossible! the queen in love with Philocles!

FLAVIA - I have suspected it before; but now
My ears and eyes are witnesses.
This hour I overheard her, to Asteria,
Making such sad complaints of her hard fate!—

For my part, I believe, you lead him back
But to his coronation.

LYSIMANTES - Hell take him first!

FLAVIA - Presently after this she called for me,
And bid me run, and, with strict care, command you,
On peril of your life, he had no harm:
But, sir, she spoke it with so great concernment,
Methought I saw love, anger, and despair,
All combating at once upon her face.

LYSIMANTES - Tell the queen,—I know not what,
I am distracted so.
But go, and leave me to my thoughts.

[Exit FLAVIA.

Was ever such amazing news,
Told in so strange and critical a moment?—
What shall I do?—
Does she love Philocles, who loves not her;
And loves not Lysimantes, who prefers her
Above his life?—What rests, but that I take
This opportunity, which she herself
Has given me, to kill this happy rival!—
Assist me, soldiers!

PHILOCLES - They shall buy me dearly.

CANDIOPE - Ah me, unhappy maid!

Enter CELADON, with his Friends, unbuttoned and reeling.

CELADON - Courage, my noble cousin! I have brought A band of blades, the bravest youths of Syracuse; Some drunk, some sober, all resolved to run Your fortune to the utmost. Fall on, mad boys!

LYSIMANTES - Hold a little!—I'm not secure of victory against these desperate ruffians.

CELADON - No, but I'll secure you! They shall cut your throat for such another word of them. Ruffians, quoth a'! call gamesters, whoremasters, and drunkards, ruffians!

LYSIMANTES - Pray, gentlemen, fall back a little.

CELADON - O ho, are they gentlemen now with you!—Speak first to your gentlemen soldiers to retire; And then I'll speak to my gentlemen ruffians. [CELADON - signs to his party. There's your disciplined men now. [They sign, and the Soldiers retire on both sides. Come, gentlemen, let's lose no time: While they are talking, let's have one merry main before we die, for mortality sake.

1ST FRIEND - Agreed! here's my cloak for a table.

2ND FRIEND - And my hat for a box.

[They lie down and throw.

LYSIMANTES - Suppose I killed him!
'Twould but exasperate the queen the more:
He loves not her, nor knows he she loves him:—
sudden thought is come into my head,—
So to contrive it, that this Philocles,
And these his friends, shall bring to pass that for me,
Which I could never compass. True, I strain
A point of honour; but then her usage to me—
It shall be so.
Pray, Philocles, command your soldiers off;
As I will mine: I've somewhat to propose,
Which you perhaps may like.

CANDIOPE - I will not leave him.

LYSIMANTES - 'Tis my desire you should not.

PHILOCLES - Cousin, lead off your friends.

CELADON - One word in your ear, coz:—Let me advise you, either make your own conditions, or never agree with him: his men are poor rogues, they can never stand before us.

[Exeunt all but LYSIMANTES, PHILOCLES and CANDIOPE.

LYSIMANTES - Suppose some friend, ere night,
Should bring you to possess all you desire;
And not so only, but secure forever
The nation's happiness?

PHILOCLES - I would think of him, As some god or angel.

LYSIMANTES - That god or angel you and I may be to one another.
We have betwixt us
An hundred men; the citadel you govern:
What were it now to seize the queen?

PHILOCLES - O impiety! to seize the queen!—
To seize her, said you?

LYSIMANTES - The word might be too rough,—I meant, secure her.

PHILOCLES - Was this your proposition?—
And had you none to make it to but me?

LYSIMANTES - Pray hear me out, ere you condemn me!—
I would not the least violence were offered

Her person. Two small grants is all I ask;
To make me happy in herself, and you
In your Candiope.

CANDIOPE - And will not you do this, my Philocles?—
Nay, now my brother speaks but reason.

PHILOCLES - Interest makes all seem reason, that leads to it.
Interest, that does the zeal of sects create,
To purge a church, and to reform a state.

LYSIMANTES - In short, the queen hath sent to part you two:—
What more she means to her, I know not.

PHILOCLES - To her, alas!—Why, will not you protect her?

LYSIMANTES - With you I can; but where's my power alone?

CANDIOPE - You know she loves me not: You lately heard her,
How she insulted over me: How she
Despised that beauty, which you say I have.
I see, she purposes my death.

PHILOCLES - Why do you fright me with it?
'Tis in your brother's power to let us 'scape,
And then you run no danger.

LYSIMANTES - True, I may;
But then my head must pay the forfeit of it.

PHILOCLES - O wretched Philocles! whither would love
Hurry thee headlong?

LYSIMANTES - Cease these exclamations.
There's no danger on your side: 'tis but to
Live without my sister; resolve that,
And you have shot the gulf.

PHILOCLES - To live without her! Is that nothing, think you?
The damned in hell endure no greater pain,
Than seeing heaven from far with hopeless eyes.

CANDIOPE - Candiope must die, and die for you:—
See it not unrevenged at least.

PHILOCLES - Ha, unrevenged! On whom should I revenge it?—
But yet she dies, and I may hinder it?
'Tis I then murder my Candiope:—
And yet, should I take arms against my queen!
That favoured me, raised me to what I am?—
Alas! it must not be.

LYSIMANTES - He cools again. [Aside.
True, she once favoured you;
But now I am informed.
She is besotted on an upstart wretch
So far, that she intends to make him master
Both of her crown and person.

PHILOCLES - Knows he that!
Then, what I dreaded most is come to pass. [Aside.
I am convinced of the necessity;
Let us make haste to raze
That action from the annals of her reign:
No motive but her glory could have wrought me.
I am a traitor to her, to preserve her
From treason to herself: Yet heaven knows,
With what a heavy heart
Philocles turns reformer. But have care
This fault of her strange passion take no air.
Let not the vulgar blow upon her fame.

LYSIMANTES - I will be careful:—Shall we go, my lord?

PHILOCLES - Time wastes apace; each first prepare his men.
Come, my Candiope.

[Exeunt PHILOCLES and CANDIOPE.

LYSIMANTES - This ruins him forever with the queen;
The odium's half his, the profit all my own.
Those who, like me, by others' help would climb,
To make them sure, must dip them in their crime.

[Exit.

SCENE II—The Queen's Apartments

Enter QUEEN and ASTERIA.

QUEEN - No more news yet from Philocles?

ASTERIA - None, madam, since Flavia's return.

QUEEN - O, my Asteria! if you loved me, sure
You would say something to me of my Philocles!
I could speak ever of him.

ASTERIA - Madam, you commanded me no more to name him to you.

QUEEN - Then I command you now, speak of nothing else:—
I charge you here, on your allegiance, tell me
What I should do with him?

ASTERIA - When you gave orders that he should be taken,
You seemed resolved how to dispose of him.

QUEEN - Dull Asteria! not to know,
Mad people never think the same thing twice!—
Alas! I'm hurried restless up and down:—
I was in anger once, and then I thought
I had put into shore:
But now a gust of love blows hard against me,
And bears me off again.

ASTERIA - Shall I sing the song, you made of Philocles,
And called it Secret Love?

QUEEN - Do; for that's all kindness. And while thou singest it,
I can think nothing but what pleases me.

SONG.
I feed a flame within, which so torments me,
That it both pains my heart, and yet contents me:
'Tis such a pleasing smart, and I so love if,
That I had rather die, than once remove it.
Yet he, for whom I grieve, shall never know it;
My tongue does not betray, nor my eyes show it.
Not a sigh, nor a tear, my pain discloses,
But they fall silently, like dew on roses.
Thus, to prevent my love from being cruel,
My heart's the sacrifice, as 'tis the fuel:
And while I suffer this to give him quiet,
My faith rewards my love, though he deny it.
On his eyes will I gaze, and there delight me;
While I conceal my love no frown can fright me:
To be more happy, I dare not aspire;
Nor can I fall more low, mounting no higher.
QUEEN - Peace!—Methinks I hear the noise
Of clashing swords, and clattering arms below.

Enter FLAVIA.

Now; what news, that you press in so rudely?

FLAVIA - Madam, the worst that can be:—
Your guards upon the sudden are surprised,
Disarmed; some slain; all scattered.

QUEEN - By whom?

FLAVIA - Prince Lysimantes, and Lord Philocles.

QUEEN - It cannot be; Philocles is a prisoner.

FLAVIA - What my eyes saw,—

QUEEN - Pull them out; they are false spectacles.

ASTERIA - O, virtue! impotent and blind as fortune!
Who would be good, or pious, if this queen,
Thy great example, suffers!

QUEEN - Peace, Asteria! accuse not virtue;
She has but given me a great occasion
Of showing what I am, when fortune leaves me.

ASTERIA - Philocles to do this!

QUEEN - Ay, Philocles!—I must confess 'twas hard!—
But there's a fate in kindness,
Still to be least returned, where most 'tis given.
Where's Candiope?

FLAVIA - Philocles was whispering to her.

QUEEN - Hence, screech-owl!—Call my guards quickly there!—
Put them apart in several prisons!—
Alas! I had forgot, I have no guards,
But those which are my jailors.
Never 'till now unhappy queen!
The use of power, till lost, is seldom known;
Now, I should strike, I find my thunder gone.

[Exeunt QUEEN and FLAVIA.

PHILOCLES enters, and meets ASTERIA going out.

PHILOCLES - Asteria, where's the queen?

ASTERIA - Ah, my lord! what have you done?
I came to seek you.

PHILOCLES - Is it from her you come?

ASTERIA - No; but on her behalf:—Her heart's too great,
In this low ebb of fortune, to entreat.

PHILOCLES - Tis but a short eclipse,
Which past, a glorious day will soon ensue.
But I would ask a favour too from you.

ASTERIA - When conquerors petition, they command:
Those, that can captive queens, who can withstand?

PHILOCLES - She, with her happiness, might mine create;
Yet seems indulgent to her own ill fate:
But she in secret hates me, sure; for why,
If not, should she Candiope deny?

ASTERIA - If you dare trust my knowledge of her mind,
She has no thoughts of you that are unkind.

PHILOCLES - I could my sorrows with some patience bear,
Did they proceed from any one but her:
But from the queen! whose person I adore,
By duty much, by inclination more.

ASTERIA - He is inclined already; did he know,
That she loved him, how would his passion grow! [Aside.

PHILOCLES - That her fair hand with destiny combines!
Fate ne'er strikes deep, but when unkindness joins:
For, to confess the secret of my mind,
Something so tender for the queen I find,
That even Candiope can scarce remove,
And, were she lower, I should call it love.

ASTERIA - She charged me, not this secret to betray;
But I best serve her, if I disobey.
For, if he loves, 'twas for her interest done;
If not, he'll keep it secret for his own. [Aside.

PHILOCLES - Why are you in obliging me so slow?

ASTERIA - The thing's of great importance, you would know;
And you must first swear secresy to all.

PHILOCLES - I swear.

ASTERIA - Yet hold; your oath's too general:
Swear that Candiope shall never know.

PHILOCLES - I swear.

ASTERIA - No; not the queen herself.

PHILOCLES - I vow.

ASTERIA - You wonder why I am so cautious grown,
In telling what concerns yourself alone:
But spare my vow, and guess what it may be,
That makes the queen deny Candiope:

'Tis neither heat, nor pride, that moves her mind;
Methinks the riddle is not hard to find.

PHILOCLES - You seem so great a wonder to intend,
As were, in me, a crime to apprehend.

ASTERIA - 'Tis not a crime to know; but would be one,
To prove ungrateful when your duty's known.

PHILOCLES - Why would you thus my easy faith abuse:
I cannot think the queen so ill would chuse.
But stay, now your imposture will appear;
She has herself confessed she loved elsewhere:
On some ignoble choice has placed her heart,
One, who wants quality, and more, desert.

ASTERIA - This, though unjust, you have most right to say;
For, if you'll rail against yourself, you may.

PHILOCLES - Dull that I was!
A thousand things now crowd my memory.
That make me know it could be none but I.
Her rage was love; and its tempestuous flame,
Like lightning, showed the heaven from whence it came.
But in her kindness my own shame I see;
Have I dethroned her, then for loving me?
I hate myself for that which I have done,
Much more, discovered, than I did unknown.
How does she brook her strange imprisonment?

ASTERIA - As great souls should, that make their own content.
The hardest term, she for your act could find,
Was only this, O Philocles, unkind!
Then, setting free a sigh, from her fair eyes
She wiped two pearls, the remnant of wild showers,
Which hung like drops upon the bells of flowers:
And thanked the heavens,
Which better did, what she designed, pursue,
Without her crime, to give her power to you.

PHILOCLES - Hold, hold! you set my thoughts so near a crown,
They mount above my reach, to pull them down:
Here constancy, ambition there does move;
On each side beauty, and on both sides love.

ASTERIA - Methinks the least you can, is to receive
This love with reverence, and your former leave.

PHILOCLES - Think but what difficulties come between!

ASTERIA - 'Tis wondrous difficult to love a queen.

PHILOCLES - For pity, cease more reasons to provide,
I am but too much yielding to your side;
And, were my heart but at my own dispose,
I should not make a scruple now to chuse.

ASTERIA - Then if the queen will my advice approve,
Her hatred to you shall expel her love.

PHILOCLES - Not to be loved by her as hard would be,
As to be hated by Candiope.

ASTERIA - I leave you to resolve while you have time;
You must be guilty, but may chuse your crime.

[Exit ASTERIA.

PHILOCLES - One thing I have resolved; and that I'll do,
Both for my love, and for my honour too;
But then (ingratitude and falsehood weighed),
I know not which would most my soul upbraid.
Fate shoves me headlong down a rugged way;
Unsafe to run, and yet too steep to stay.

[Exit PHILOCLES.

ACT V

SCENE I—The Court

FLORIMEL in man's habit.

Flor. 'Twill be rare now, if I can go through with it, to outdo this mad Celadon in all his tricks, and get both his mistresses from him; then I shall revenge myself upon all three, and save my own stake into the bargain; for I find I do love the rogue, in spite of all his infidelities. Yonder they are, and this way they must come. If clothes and a bon mien will take them, I shall do it. Save you, Monsieur Florimel! Faith, me thinks you are a very janty fellow, poudré et ajusté, as well as the best of 'em. I can manage the little comb; set my hat, shake my garniture, toss about my empty noddle, walk with a courant slur, and at every step peck down my head: If I should be mistaken for some courtier now, pray where's the difference?

Enter, to her, CELADON, OLINDA, and SABINA.

OLINDA - Never mince the matter!

SABRINA - You have left your heart behind with Florimel; we know it.

CELADON - You know you wrong me: when I am with Florimel, 'tis still your prisoner, it only draws a longer chain after it.

FLORIMEL - Is it e'en so! then farewell, poor Florimel! thy maidenhead is condemned to die with thee.

CELADON - But let's leave this discourse; 'tis all digression, that does not speak of your beauties.

FLORIMEL - Now for me, in the name of impudence!—[Comes forward.] They are the greatest beauties, I confess, that ever I beheld—

CELADON - How now, what's the meaning of this young fellow?

FLORIMEL - And therefore I cannot wonder that this gentleman, who has the honour to be known to you, should admire you, since I, that am a stranger—

CELADON - And a very impudent one, as I take it, sir.

FLORIMEL - Am so extremely surprised, that I admire, love, am wounded, and am dying, all in a moment.

CELADON - I have seen him somewhere, but where I know not:—Pry'thee, my friend, leave us; dost thou think, we do not know our way in court?

FLORIMEL - I pretend not to instruct you in your way; you see I do not go before you; but you cannot possibly deny me the happiness to wait upon these ladies; me, who—

CELADON - Thee, who shalt be beaten most unmercifully, if thou dost follow them.

FLORIMEL - You will not draw in court, I hope?

CELADON - Pox on him, let's walk away faster, and be rid of him.

FLORIMEL - O, take no care for me, sir! you shall not lose me; I'll rather mend my pace, than not wait on you.

OLINDA - I begin to like this fellow.

CELADON - You make very bold here in my seraglio, and I shall find a time to tell you so, sir.

FLORIMEL - When you find a time to tell me on't, I shall find a time to answer you: But, pray, what do you find in yourself so extraordinary, that you should serve these ladies better than I? Let me know what 'tis you value yourself upon, and let them judge betwixt us.

CELADON - I am somewhat more a man than you.

FLORIMEL - That is, you are so much older than I:—Do you like a man ever the better for his age, ladies?

SABRINA - Well said, young-gentleman.

CELADON - Pish, thee! a young raw creature; thou hast ne'er been under the barber's hands yet.

FLORIMEL - No, nor under the surgeon's neither, as you have been.

CELADON - 'Slife, what would'st thou be at? I am madder than thou art.

FLORIMEL - The devil you are! I'll tope with you; I'll sing with you;
I'll dance with you;—I'll swagger with you—

CELADON - I'll fight with you.

FLORIMEL - Out upon fighting; 'tis grown so common a fashion, that a modish man condemns it; a man of garniture and feather is above the dispensation of the sword.

OLINDA - Uds my life! here's the queen's music just going to us; you shall decide your quarrel by a dance.

SABRINA - Who stops the fiddles?

CELADON - Base and treble, by your leaves, we arrest you at these ladies' suits.

FLORIMEL - Come on, sirs, play me a jig; you shall see how I'll baffle him.

DANCE.

FLORIMEL - Your judgment, ladies.

OLINDA - You, sir; you, sir: This is the rarest gentleman! I could live and die with him—

SABRINA - Lord, how he sweats! please you, sir, to make use of my handkerchief?

OLINDA - You and I are merry, and just of an humour, sir; therefore we two should love one another.

SABRINA - And you and I are just of an age, sir; and therefore, methinks, we should not hate one another.

CELADON - Then I perceive, ladies, I am a castaway, a reprobate, with you: Why, 'faith, this is hard luck now, that I should be no less than one whole hour in getting your affections, and now must lose 'em in a quarter of it.

OLINDA - No matter, let him rail; does the loss afflict you, sir?

CELADON - No, in faith, does it not; for if you had not forsaken me, I had you: So the willows may flourish, for any branches I shall rob 'em of.

SABRINA - However, we have the advantage to have left you; not you us.

CELADON - That's only a certain nimbleness in nature, you women have, to be first inconstant; but if you had not made the more haste, the wind was veering too upon my weathercock: The best on't is, Florimel is worth both of you.

FLORIMEL - 'Tis like she'll accept of their leavings.

CELADON - She will accept on't, and she shall accept on't: I think I know more than you of her mind, sir.

Enter MELISSA.

MELISSA - Daughters, there's a poor collation within, that waits for you.

FLORIMEL - Will you walk, musty sir?

CELADON - No, marry, sir, I will not; I have surfeited of that old woman's face already.

FLORIMEL - Begin some frolic, then; what will you do for her?

CELADON - Faith, I am no dog, to show tricks for her; I cannot come aloft to an old woman.

FLORIMEL - Dare you kiss her?

CELADON - I was never dared by any man. By your leave, old madam— [He plucks off her ruff.

MELISSA - Help! help! do you discover my nakedness?

CELADON - Peace, Tiffany! no harm! [He puts on the ruff.] Now, Sir, here's Florimel's health to you. [Kisses her.

MELISSA - Away, sir!—A sweet young man as you are, to abuse the gift of nature so!

CELADON - Good mother, do not commend me so; I am flesh and blood, and you do not know what you may pluck upon that reverend person of yours. Come on, follow your leader.

[Gives FLORIMEL the ruff; she puts it on.

FLORIMEL - Stand fair, mother—

CELADON - What, with your hat on? Lie thou there;—and thou, too—

[Plucks off her hat and peruke, and discovers FLORIMEL.

ALL - Florimel!

FLORIMEL - My kind mistresses, how sorry I am, I can do you no further service! I think I had best resign you to Celadon, to make amends for me.

CELADON - Lord! what a misfortune it was, ladies, that the gentleman could not hold forth to you?

OLINDA - We have lost Celadon too.

MELISSA - Come away; this is past enduring. [Exeunt MELISSA and OLINDA.

SABRINA - Well, if ever I believe a man to be a man, for the sake of a peruke and feather again.

FLORIMEL - Come, Celadon, shall we make accounts even? Lord! what a hanging-look was there? indeed, if you had been recreant to your mistress, or had forsworn your love, that sinner's face had been but decent; but, for the virtuous, the innocent, the constant Celadon!

CELADON - This is not very heroic in you now, to insult over a man in his misfortunes; but take heed, you have robb'd me of my two mistresses; I shall grow desperately constant, and all the tempest of my love will fall upon your head: I shall so pay you!—

FLORIMEL - Who, you pay me! you are a bankrupt, cast beyond all possibility of recovery.

CELADON - If I am a bankrupt, I'll be a very honest one; when I cannot pay my debts, at least I'll give you up the possession of my body.

FLORIMEL - No, I'll deal better with you; since you are unable to pay, I'll give in your bond.

Enter PHILOCLES with a commanders staff in his hand, attended.

PHILOCLES - Cousin, I am sorry I must take you from your company about an earnest business.

FLORIMEL - There needs no excuse, my lord; we had despatched our affairs, and were just parting.

CELADON - Will you be going, sir? sweet sir,—damn'd sir!—I have but one word more to say to you.

FLORIMEL - As I am a man of honour, I'll wait on you some other time.

CELADON - By these breeches,—

FLORIMEL - Which, if I marry you, I am resolved to wear; put that into our bargain, and so adieu, sir.

[Exit FLORIMEL.

PHILOCLES - Hark you, cousin,—[They whisper. You'll see it exactly executed; I rely upon you.

CELADON - I shall not fail, my lord; may the conclusion of it prove happy to you. [Exit CELADON.

PHILOCLES solus.
Wheree'er I cast about my wandering eyes,
Greatness lies ready in some shape to tempt me.
The royal furniture in every room,
The guards, and the huge waving crowds of people,
All waiting for a sight of that fair queen,
Who makes a present of her love to me:
Now tell me, Stoick!
If all these with a wish might be made thine,
Would'st thou not truck thy ragged virtue for 'em?
If glory was a bait, that angels swallow'd,
How then should souls allied to sense resist it?

Enter CANDIOPE.

Ah poor Candiope! I pity her,

But that is all.

CANDIOPE - O my dear Philocles!
A thousand blessings wait on thee!
The hope of being thine, I think, will put
Me past my meat and sleep with ecstasy,
So I shall keep the fasts of seraphims,
And wake for joy, like nightingales in May.

PHILOCLES - Wake, Philocles, wake from thy dream of glory,
'Tis all but shadow to Candiope:
Canst thou betray a love so innocent? [Aside.

CANDIOPE - What makes you melancholick? I doubt,
I have displeased you.

PHILOCLES - No, my love, I am not displeased with you,
But with myself, when I consider,
How little I deserve you.

CANDIOPE - Say not so, my Philocles; a love so true as yours,
That would have left a court, and a queen's favour,
To live in a poor hermitage with me,—

PHILOCLES - Ha! she has stung me to the quick!
As if she knew the falsehood I intended:
But, I thank heaven, it has recall'd my virtue;
[Aside.
Oh! my dear, I love you, and you only; [To her.
Go in, I have some business for a while;
But I think minutes ages till we meet.

CANDIOPE - I knew you had; but yet I could not chuse,
But come and look upon you.

[Exit CANDIOPE.

PHILOCLES - What barbarous man would wrong so sweet a virtue!

Enter the QUEEN in black, with ASTERIA.

Madam, the states are straight to meet; but why
In these dark ornaments will you be seen?

QUEEN - They fit the fortune of a captive queen.

PHILOCLES - Deep shades are thus to heighten colours set;
So stars in night, and diamonds shine in jet.

QUEEN - True friends should so in dark afflictions shine,
But I have no great cause to boast of mine.

PHILOCLES - You may have too much prejudice for some,
And think them false, before their trials come.
But, madam, what determine you to do?

QUEEN - I came not here to be advised by you:
But charge you, by that power which once you owned,
And which is still my right, even when unthroned,
That whatsoe'er the states resolve of me,
You never more think of Candiope.

PHILOCLES - Not think of her! ah, how should I obey!
Her tyrant eyes have forced my heart away.

QUEEN - By force retake it from those tyrant eyes,
I'll grant you out my letters of reprise.

PHILOCLES - She has too well prevented that design,
By giving me her heart, in change for mine.

QUEEN - Thus foolish Indians gold for glass forego;
'Twas to your loss you prized your heart so low.
I set its value when you were advanced,
And as my favours grew, its rate enhanced.

PHILOCLES - The rate of subjects' hearts by yours must go,
And love in yours has set the value low.

QUEEN - I stand corrected, and myself reprove;
You teach me to repent my low-placed love:
Help me this passion from my heart to tear!—
Now rail on him, and I will sit and hear.

PHILOCLES - Madam, like you, I have repented too,
And dare not rail on one, I do not know.

QUEEN - This, Philocles, like strange perverseness shews,
As if whate'er I said you would oppose;
How come you thus concerned for this unknown?

PHILOCLES - I only judge his actions by my own.

QUEEN - I've heard too much, and you too much have said.
O heavens, the secret of my soul's betrayed!
He knows my love, I read it in his face,
And blushes, conscious of his queen's disgrace.
[Aside.
Hence quickly, hence, or I shall die with shame.
[To him.

PHILOCLES - Now I love both, and both with equal flame.

Wretched I came, more wretched I retire:
When two winds blow it, who can quench the fire?

[Exit PHILOCLES.

QUEEN - O my Asteria! I know not whom to accuse;
But either my own eyes, or you, have told
My love to Philocles.

ASTERIA - Is't possible that he should know it, madam?

QUEEN - Methinks, you ask that question guiltily.
[Lays her hand on ASTERIA'S shoulder.
Confess, for I will know, what was the subject
Of your long discourse i'th' antichamber with him.

ASTERIA - It was business to convince him, madam,
How ill he did, being so much obliged,
To join in your imprisonment.

QUEEN - Nay, now I am confirmed my thought was true;
For you could give him no such reason
Of his obligements, as my love.

ASTERIA - Because I saw him much a malecontent,
I thought to win him to your interest, madam,
By telling him it was no want of kindness,
Made your refusal of Candiope.
And he, perhaps—

QUEEN - What of him now?

ASTERIA - As men are apt, interpreted my words,
To all the advantage he could wrest the sense,
As if I meant you loved him.

QUEEN - Have I deposited within thy breast
The dearest treasure of my life, my glory,
And hast thou thus betrayed me!
But why do I accuse thy female weakness,
And not my own, for trusting thee!
Unhappy queen, Philocles knows thy fondness,
And needs must think it done by thy command.

ASTERIA - Dear madam, think not so.

QUEEN - Peace, peace, thou should'st for ever hold thy tongue:
For it has spoke too much for all thy life. [To her.
Then Philocles has told Candiope,
And courts her kindness with his scorn of me.
O whither am I fallen!

But I must rouse myself, and give a stop
To all these ills by headlong passion caused.
In hearts resolved weak love is put to flight,
And only conquers, when we dare not fight.
But we indulge our harms, and, while he gains
An entrance, please ourselves into our pains.

Enter LYSIMANTES.

ASTERIA - Prince Lysimantes, madam.

QUEEN - Come near, you poor deluded criminal;
See how ambition cheats you:
You thought to find a prisoner here,
But you behold a queen.

LYSIMANTES - And may you long be so! 'tis true, this act
May cause some wonder in your majesty.

QUEEN - None, cousin, none; I ever thought you
Ambitious, proud, designing.

LYSIMANTES - Yet all my pride, designs, and my ambition,
Were taught me by a master,
With whom you are not unacquainted, madam.

QUEEN - Explain yourself; dark purposes, like yours,
Need an interpretation.

LYSIMANTES - 'Tis love, I mean.

QUEEN - Have my low fortunes given thee
This insolence, to name it to thy queen?

LYSIMANTES - Yet you have heard, love named without offence.
As much below you as you think my passion,
I can look down on yours.

QUEEN - Does he know it too!
This is the extremest malice of my stars! [Aside.

LYSIMANTES - You see that princes' faults,
(Howe'er they think them safe from public view)
Fly out thro the dark crannies of their closets:
We know what the sun does,
Even when we see him not, in t'other world.

QUEEN - My actions, cousin, never feared the light.

LYSIMANTES - Produce him, then, your darling of the dark.
For such an one you have.

QUEEN - I know no such.

LYSIMANTES - You know, but will not own him.

QUEEN - Rebels ne'er want pretence to blacken kings,
And this, it seems, is yours: Do you produce him,
Or ne'er hereafter sully my renown
With this aspersion:—Sure he dare not name him.
[Aside.

LYSIMANTES - I am too tender of your frame; or else—
Nor are things brought to that extremity:
Provided you accept my passion,
I'll gladly yield to think I was deceived.

QUEEN - Keep in your error still; I will not buy
Your good opinion at so dear a rate,
And my own misery, by being yours.

LYSIMANTES - Do not provoke my patience by such scorns.
For fear I break through all, and name him to you.

QUEEN - Hope not to fright me with your mighty looks;
Know, I dare stem that tempest in your brow,
And dash it back upon you.

LYSIMANTES - Spite of prudence it will out:—'Tis Philocles!
Now judge, when I was made a property
To cheat myself, by making him your prisoner,
Whether I had not right to take up arms?

QUEEN - Poor envious wretch!
Was this the venom that swelled up thy breast?
My grace to Philocles mis-deemed my love!

LYSIMANTES - Tis true, the gentleman is innocent;
He ne'er sinned up so high, not in his wishes;
You know he loves elsewhere.

QUEEN - You mean your sister.

LYSIMANTES - I wish some Sibyl now would tell me,
Why you refused her to him.

QUEEN - Perhaps I did not think him worthy of her.

LYSIMANTES - Did you not think him too worthy, madam?
This is too thin a veil to hide your passion;
To prove you love him not, yet give her him,
And I'll engage my honour to lay down my arms.

QUEEN - He is arrived where I would wish—
[Aside.
Call in the company, and you shall see what I will do.

LYSIMANTES - Who waits without there? [Exit LYS.

QUEEN - Now hold, my heart, for this one act of honour,
And I will never ask more courage of thee:
Once more I have the means to reinstate myself into my glory.
I feel my love to Philocles within me
Shrink, and pull back my heart from this hard trial.
But it must be, when glory says it must:
As children, wading from some river's bank,
First try the water with their tender feet;
Then, shuddering up with cold, step back again,
And straight a little further venture on,
Till, at the last, they plunge into the deep,
And pass, at once, what they were doubting long:
I'll make the experiment; it shall be done in haste,
Because I'll put it past my power to undo.
Enter at one door LYSIMANTES, at the other PHILOCLES, CELADON, CANDIOPE, FLORIMEL, FLAVIA,
OLINDA, SABINA, the three deputies, and soldiers.

LYSIMANTES - In arms! is all well, Philocles?

PHILOCLES - No, but it shall be.

QUEEN - He comes, and with him
The fever of my love returns to shake me.
I see love is not banished from my soul;
He is still there, but is chained up by glory.

ASTERIA - You've made a noble conquest, madam.

QUEEN - Come hither Philocles: I am first to tell you,
I and my cousin are agreed; he has
Engaged to lay down arms.

PHILOCLES - 'Tis well for him he has; for all his party,
By my command, already are surprised,
While I was talking with your majesty.

CELADON - Yes, 'faith, I have done him that courtesy;
I brought his followers, under pretence of guarding
it, to a strait place, where they are all coupt up
without use of their arms, and may be pelted to
death by the small infantry o'er the town.

QUEEN - 'Twas more than I expected, or could hope;
Yet still I thought your meaning honest.

PHILOCLES - My fault was rashness, but 'twas full of zeal:
Nor had I e'er been led to that attempt,
Had I not seen, it would be done without me:
But by compliance I preserved the power,
Which I have since made use of for your service.

QUEEN - And which I purpose so to recompence—

LYSIMANTES - With her crown, she means: I knew 'twould come to it.
[Aside.

PHILOCLES - O heavens, she'll own her love!
Then I must lose Candiope for ever,
And, floating in a vast abyss of glory,
Seek and not find myself!—

QUEEN - Take your Candiope; and be as happy
As love can make you both:—How pleased I am,
That I can force my tongue
To speak words, so far distant from my heart!
[Aside.

CANDIOPE - My happiness is more than I can utter!

LYSIMANTES - Methinks I could do violence on myself, for taking arms
Against a queen, so good, so bountiful:
Give me leave, madam, in my ecstasy
Of joy, to give you thanks for Philocles:—
You have preserved my friend, and now he owes not
His fortunes only to your favour; but,
What's more, his life, and, more than that, his love.
I am convinced, she never loved him now;
Since by her free consent, all force removed,
She gives him to my sister.
Flavia was an impostor, and deceived me. [Aside.

PHILOCLES - As for me, madam, I can only say,
That I beg respite for my thanks; for, on a sudden,
The benefit's so great, it overwhelms me.

ASTERIA - Mark but the faintness of the acknowledgement.
[To the Queen, aside.

QUEEN to ASTERIA] I have observed it with you, and am pleased,
He seems not satisfied; for I still wish
That he may love me.

PHILOCLES - I see Asteria deluded me,
With flattering hopes of the queen's love.
Only to draw me off from Lysimantes:

But I will think no more on't.
I'm going to possess Candiope,
And I am ravished with the joy on't!—ha!
Not ravished neither.
For what can be more charming than that queen!
Behold how night sits lovely on her eye-brows,
While day breaks from her eyes! then a crown too:
Lost, lost, for ever lost; and now 'tis gone,
Tis beautiful. [Aside.

ASTERIA - How he eyes you still! [To the QUEEN.

PHILOCLES - Sure I had one of the fallen angels' dreams;
All heaven within this hour was mine! [Aside.

CANDIOPE - What is it, that disturbs you, dear?

PHILOCLES - Only the greatness of my joy:
I've ta'en too strong a cordial, love,
And cannot yet digest it.

QUEEN - Tis done!
[Clapping her hand on ASTERIA,
But this pang more, and then a glorious birth.
The tumults of this day, my loyal subjects,
Have settled in my heart a resolution,
Happy for you, and glorious too for me.
First, for my cousin; tho', attempting on my person,
He has incurred the danger of the laws,
I will not punish him.

LYSIMANTES - You bind me ever to my loyalty.

QUEEN - Then that I may oblige you more to it,
I here declare you rightful successor,
And heir immediate to my crown:
This, gentlemen—[To the deputies.
I hope will still my subjects' discontents,
When they behold succession firmly settled.

Dep. Heaven preserve your majesty!

QUEEN - As for myself, I have resolved
Still to continue as I am, unmarried:
The cares, observances, and all the duties
Which I should pay an husband, I will place
Upon my people; and our mutual love
Shall make a blessing more than conjugal,
And this the states shall ratify.

LYSIMANTES - Heaven bear me witness, that I take no joy

In the succession of a crown,
Which must descend to me so sad a way.

QUEEN - Cousin, no more; my resolution's past
Which fate shall never alter.

PHILOCLES - Then I am once more happy;
For, since none must possess her, I am pleased
With my own choice, and will desire no more:
For multiplying wishes is a curse.
That keeps the mind still painfully awake.

QUEEN - Celadon.
Your care and loyalty have this day obliged me;
But how to be acknowledging, I know not,
Unless you give the means.

CELADON - I was in hope your majesty had forgot me; therefore, if you please, madam, I'll only beg a pardon for having taken up arms once to-day against you; for I have a foolish kind of conscience, which I wish many of your subjects had, that will not let me ask a recompence for my loyalty, when I know I have been a rebel.

QUEEN - Your modesty shall not serve the turn; ask something.

CELADON - Then I beg, madam, you will command Florimel never to be friends with me.

FLORIMEL - Ask again; I grant that without the queen:
But why are you afraid on't?

CELADON - Because I am sure, as soon as ever you are, you'll marry me.

FLORIMEL - Do you fear it?

CELADON - No, 'twill come with a fear.

FLORIMEL - If you do, I will not stick with you for an oath.

CELADON - I require no oath till we come to church: and then after the priest, I hope; for I find it will be my destiny to marry thee.

FLORIMEL - If ever I say a word after the black gentleman for thee, Celadon—

CELADON - Then, I hope, you'll give me leave to bestow a faithful heart elsewhere.

FLORIMEL - Ay, but if you would have one, you must bespeak it, for I am sure you have none ready made.

CELADON - What say you, shall I marry Flavia?

FLORIMEL - No, she'll be too cunning for you.

CELADON - What say you to Olinda, then? she's tall, and fair, and bonny.

FLORIMEL - And foolish, and apish, and fickle.

CELADON - But Sabina there's pretty, and young, and loving, and innocent.

FLORIMEL - And dwarfish, and childish, and fond, and flippant: If you marry her sister, you will get may-poles; and if you marry her, you will get fairies to dance about them.

CELADON - Nay, then, the case is clear, Florimel; if you take 'em all from me, 'tis because you reserve me for yourself.

FLORIMEL - But this marriage is such a bugbear to me! much might be if we could invent but any way to make it easy.

CELADON - Some foolish people have made it uneasy, by drawing the knot faster than they need; but we that are wiser will loosen it a little.

FLORIMEL - 'Tis true, indeed, there's some difference betwixt a girdle and a halter.

CELADON - As for the first year, according to the laudable custom of new-married people, we shall follow one another up into chambers, and down into gardens, and think we shall never have enough of one another. So far 'tis pleasant enough, I hope.

FLORIMEL - But after that, when we begin to live like husband and wife, and never come near one another—what then, sir?

CELADON - Why, then, our only happiness must be to have one mind, and one will, Florimel.

FLORIMEL - One mind, if thou wilt, but pr'ythee let us have two wills; for I find one will be little enough for me alone. But how, if those wills should meet and clash, Celadon?

CELADON - I warrant thee for that; husbands and wives keep their wills far enough asunder for ever meeting. One thing let us be sure to agree on, that is, never to be jealous.

FLORIMEL - No; but e'en love one another as long as we can; and confess the truth when we can love no longer.

CELADON - When I have been at play, you shall never ask me what money I have lost.

FLORIMEL - When I have been abroad, you shall never enquire who treated me.

CELADON - Item, I will have the liberty to sleep all night, without your interrupting my repose for any evil design whatsoever.

FLORIMEL - Item, Then you shall bid me goodnight before you sleep.

CELADON - Provided always, that whatever liberties we take with other people, we continue very honest to one another.

FLORIMEL - As far as will consist with a pleasant life.

CELADON - Lastly, whereas the names of husband and wife hold forth nothing, but clashing and cloying, and dulness and faintness, in their signification; they shall be abolished for ever betwixt us.

FLORIMEL - And instead of those, we will be married by the more agreeable names of mistress and gallant.

CELADON - None of my privileges to be infringed by thee, Florimel, under the penalty of a month of fasting nights.

FLORIMEL - None of my privileges to be infringed by thee, Celadon, under the penalty of cuckoldom.

CELADON - Well, if it be my fortune to be made a cuckold, I had rather thou should'st make me one, than any one in Sicily; and, for my comfort, I shall have thee oftener than any of thy servants.

FLORIMEL - Look ye now, is not such a marriage as good as wenching, Celadon?

CELADON - This is very good; but not so good, Florimel.

QUEEN - Now set we forward to the assembly. You promise, cousin, your consent?

LYSIMANTES - But most unwillingly.

QUEEN - Philocles, I must beg your voice too.

PHILOCLES - Most joyfully I give it.

LYSIMANTES - Madam, but one word more;—
Since you are so resolved,
That you may see, bold as my passion was,
'Twas only for your person, not your crown;
I swear no second love
Shall violate the flame I had for you,
But, in strict imitation of your oath,
I vow a single life.

QUEEN - Now, my Asteria, my joys are full;
[To ASTERIA.
The powers above, that see
The innocent love I bear to Philocles,
Have given its due reward; for by this means
The right of Lysimantes will devolve
Upon Candiope: and I shall have
This great content, to think, when I am dead,
My crown may fall on Philocles's head.

[Exeunt.

EPILOGUE

Our poet, something doubtful of his fate,
Made choice of me to be his advocate,
Relying on my knowledge in the laws;
And I as boldly undertook the cause.
I left my client yonder in a rant,
Against the envious, and the ignorant,
Who are, he says, his only enemies:
But he condemns their malice, and defies
The sharpest of his censurers to say,
Where there is one gross fault in all his play.
The language is so fitted for each part,
The plot according to the rules of art,
And twenty other things he bid me tell you;
But I cried, e'en go do't yourself for Nelly.[A]
Reason with judges, urged in the defence
Of those they would condemn, is insolence;
I therefore wave the merits of his play,
And think it fit to plead this safer way.
If when too many in the purchase share,
Robbing's not worth the danger nor the care;
The men of business must, in policy,
Cherish a little harmless poetry,
All wit would else grow up to knavery.
Wit is a bird of music, or of prey;
Mounting, she strikes at all things in her way.
But if this birdlime once but touch her wings,
On the next bush she sits her down and sings.
I have but one word more; tell me, I pray,
What you will get by damning of our play?
A whipt fanatic, who does not recant,
Is, by his brethren, called a suffering saint;
And by your hands should this poor poet die,
Before he does renounce his poetry,
His death must needs confirm the party more,
Than all his scribbling life could do before;
Where so much zeal does in a sect appear,
'Tis to no purpose, 'faith, to be severe.
But t'other day, I heard this rhyming fop
Say,—Critics were the whips, and he the top;
For, as a top spins more, the more you baste her,
So, every lash you give, he writes the faster.

[Footnote A: The epilogue appears to have been spoken by Nell Gwynn.]

PROLOGUE

SPOKEN BY MRS BOUTELL TO THE MAIDEN QUEEN, IN MAN'S CLOTHES.

The following prologue and epilogue occur in the "Covent-Garden Drollery" a publication which contains original copies of several of Dryden's fugitive pieces. They appear to have been spoken upon occasion of the male characters in "The Maiden Queen" being represented by female performers. From our author's connection both with the play and with Mrs Reeves, who spoke the epilogue, it is probable he wrote both that and the prologue; and therefore (although not much worth preserving) we have here added them. From the reference to Ravenscroft's play of "The Citizen turned Gentleman," in the last line of the epilogue, it would seem the prologue and epilogue were written and spoken in 1672.

Women, like us, (passing for men,) you'll cry,
Presume too much upon your secrecy.
There's not a fop in town, but will pretend
To know the cheat himself, or by his friend;
Then make no words on't, gallants, 'tis e'en true,
We are condemn'd to look and strut, like you.
Since we thus freely our hard fate confess,
Accept us, these bad times, in any dress.
You'll find the sweet on't: now old pantaloons
Will go as far as, formerly, new gowns;
And from your own cast wigs, expect no frowns.
The ladies we shall not so easily please;
They'll say,—What impudent bold things are these,
That dare provoke, yet cannot do us right,
Like men, with huffing looks, that dare not fight!—
But this reproach our courage must not daunt;
The bravest soldier may a weapon want;
Let her that doubts us still send her gallant.
Ladies, in us you'll youth and beauty find:
All things—but one—according to your mind:
And when your eyes and ears are feasted here,
Rise up, and make out the short meal elsewhere.

EPILOGUE

SPOKEN BY MRS REEVES TO THE MAIDEN QUEEN, IN MAN'S CLOTHES.

What think you, sirs, was't not all well enough?
Will you not grant that we can strut and huff?
Men may be proud; but faith, for aught I see,
They neither walk, nor cock, so well as we;
And, for the fighting part, we may in time
Grow up to swagger in heroic rhyme;
For though we cannot boast of equal force,
Yet, at some weapons, men have still the worse.
Why should not then we women act alone?
Or whence are men so necessary grown?
Our's are so old, they are as good as none.
Some who have tried them, if you'll take their oaths,

Swear they're as arrant tinsel as their clothes.
Imagine us but what we represent,
And we could e'en give you as good content.
Our faces, shapes,—all's better then you see,
And for the rest, they want as much as we.
Oh, would the higher powers behind to us,
And grant us to set up a female house!
We'll make ourselves to please both sexes then,—
To the men women, to the women men.
Here, we presume, our legs are no ill sight,
And they will give you no ill dreams at night:
In dreams both sexes may their passions ease,
You make us then as civil as you please.
This would prevent the houses joining too,
At which we are as much displeased as you;
For all our women most devoutly swear,
Each would be rather a poor actress here,
Then to be made a Mamamouchi there.

John Dryden – A Short Biography

John Dryden was born on August 9th, 1631 in the village rectory of Aldwincle near Thrapston in Northamptonshire, where his maternal grandfather was Rector of All Saints Church.

Dryden was the eldest of fourteen children born to Erasmus Dryden and wife Mary Pickering, paternal grandson of Sir Erasmus Dryden, 1st Baronet (1553–1632) and wife Frances Wilkes, Puritan landowning gentry who supported the Puritan cause and Parliament.

As a boy Dryden lived in the nearby village of Titchmarsh, Northamptonshire where it is probable that he received his first education.

In 1644 he was sent to Westminster School as a King's Scholar where his headmaster was Dr. Richard Busby, a charismatic teacher but severe disciplinarian. Having recently been re-founded by Elizabeth I, Westminster now embraced a very different religious and political spirit encouraging royalism and high Anglicanism but as a humanist public school, it maintained a curriculum which trained pupils in the art of rhetoric and the presentation of arguments for both sides of a given issue. This skill would remain with Dryden and influence his later writing and thinking, as much of it displays these dialectical patterns.

His first published poem, whilst still at Westminster, was an elegy with a strong royalist flavour on the death of his schoolmate Henry, Lord Hastings from smallpox, and alludes to the execution of King Charles I, which took place on January 30th, 1649.

In 1650 Dryden was ready for University and travelled to Trinity College, Cambridge. Dryden's undergraduate years would almost certainly have followed the standard curriculum of classics, rhetoric, and mathematics.

Dryden obtained his BA in 1654, graduating top of the list for Trinity that year.

However family tragedy struck in June of the same year when Dryden's father died, leaving him some land which generated a small income, but not enough to live on.

Returning to London during The Protectorate, Dryden now obtained work with Cromwell's Secretary of State, John Thurloe. This may have been the result of influence exercised on his behalf by his cousin the Lord Chamberlain, Sir Gilbert Pickering.

At Cromwell's funeral on 23 November 1658 Dryden was in the company of the Puritan poets John Milton and Andrew Marvell. The setting was to be a sea change in English history. From Republic to Monarchy and from one set of lauded poets to what would soon become the Age of Dryden.

The start began later that year when Dryden published the first of his great poems, Heroic Stanzas (1658), a eulogy on Cromwell's death which is necessarily cautious and prudent in its emotional display.

With the Restoration of the Monarchy in 1660 Dryden celebrated in verse with Astraea Redux, an authentic royalist panegyric. In this work the interregnum is illustrated as a time of anarchy, and Charles is seen as the restorer of peace and order.

With the king now established Dryden moved quickly to place himself as the leading poet and critic of his day and transferred his allegiances to the new government.

Along with Astraea Redux, Dryden welcomed the new regime with two more panegyrics: To His Sacred Majesty: A Panegyric on his Coronation (1662) and To My Lord Chancellor (1662).

These panegyrics are occasional and written to celebrate events. Thus they are written for the nation rather than the self, but these and others put him in good standing for his eventual appointment as Poet Laureate, where a number of event poems would be required each year and speaking for the Nation and to the Nation would be the first order of duty.

These poems suggest that Dryden was looking to court a possible patron which would have given him an income and time to explore his creative ideas but no, his path instead would be to make a living in writing for publishers, not for the aristocracy, and thus ultimately for the reading public.

In November 1662 Dryden was proposed for membership in the Royal Society, and he was elected an early fellow. However, his inactivity and non payment of dues led to his expulsion in 1666.

On December 1st, 1663 Dryden married the Royalist sister of Sir Robert Howard—Lady Elizabeth Howard (died 1714). The marriage was at St. Swithin's, London, and the consent of the parents is noted on the license, though Lady Elizabeth was then about twenty-five. She was the object of some scandals, well or ill founded; it was said that Dryden had been bullied into the marriage by her brothers. A small estate in Wiltshire was settled upon them by her father. The lady's intellect and temper were apparently not good; her husband was treated as an inferior by those of her social status.

Dryden's works occasionally contain outbursts against the married state but also celebrations of the same. Little else is known of the intimate side of his marriage.

Both Dryden and his wife were warmly attached to their children. They had three sons: Charles (1666–1704), John (1668–1701), and Erasmus Henry (1669–1710). Lady Elizabeth Dryden survived her husband, but went insane soon after his death and died in 1714.

With the re-opening of the theatres after the Puritan ban, Dryden began to also write plays. His first play, The Wild Gallant, appeared in 1663 but was not successful. From 1668 on he was contracted to produce three plays a year for the King's Company, in which he became a shareholder. During the 1660s and '70s, theatrical writing was his main source of income. He led the way in Restoration comedy, his best-known works being Marriage à la Mode (1672), as well as heroic tragedy and regular tragedy, in which his greatest success was All for Love (1678). Dryden was never fully satisfied with his theatrical writings and frequently suggested that his talents were wasted on unworthy audiences.

Certainly therefore fame as a poet looked more rewarding. In 1667, around the same time his dramatic career began, he published Annus Mirabilis, a lengthy historical poem which described the English defeat of the Dutch naval fleet and the Great Fire of London in 1666. It was a modern epic in pentameter quatrains that established him as the pre-eminent poet of his generation, and was crucial in his attaining the posts of Poet Laureate (1668) and then historiographer royal (1670).

When the Great Plague of London closed the theatres in 1665 Dryden retreated to Wiltshire where he wrote Of Dramatick Poesie (1668), arguably the best of his unsystematic prefaces and essays. Dryden constantly defended his own literary practice, and Of Dramatick Poesie, the longest of his critical works, takes the form of a dialogue in which four characters—each based on a prominent contemporary, with Dryden himself as 'Neander'—debate the merits of classical, French and English drama.

He felt strongly about the relation of the poet to tradition and the creative process, and his heroic play Aureng-zebe (1675) has a prologue which denounces the use of rhyme in serious drama. His play All for Love (1678) was written in blank verse, and was to immediately follow Aureng-Zebe.

On December 18th, 1679 he was attacked in Rose Alley near his home in Covent Garden by thugs hired by fellow poet, John Wilmot, 2nd Earl of Rochester, with whom he had a long-standing conflict. Wilmot was constantly in and out of favour with the King and his own poetry was often bawdy, lewd, even obscene and made fun of the King who would often exile him from Court.

Dryden's greatest achievements were in satiric verse: the mock-heroic Mac Flecknoe, a more personal product of his Laureate years, was a lampoon circulated in manuscript and an attack on the playwright Thomas Shadwell. Dryden's main goal in the work is to "satirize Shadwell, ostensibly for his offenses against literature but more immediately we may suppose for his habitual badgering of him on the stage and in print." It is not a belittling form of satire, but rather one which makes his object great in ways which are unexpected, transferring the ridiculous into poetry. This line of satire continued with Absalom and Achitophel (1681) and The Medal (1682). Other major works from this period are the religious poems Religio Laici (1682), written from the position of a member of the Church of England; his 1683 edition of Plutarch's Lives, translated From the Greek by Several Hands in which he introduced the word biography to English readers; and The Hind and the Panther, (1687) which celebrates his conversion to Roman Catholicism.

He wrote Britannia Rediviva celebrating the birth of a son and heir to the Catholic King and Queen on June 10th, 1688. When later in the same year James II was deposed in the Glorious Revolution, Dryden's refusal to take the oaths of allegiance to the new monarchs, William and Mary, which left him out of favour at court and he had to leave his post as Poet Laureate. Thomas Shadwell, his despised rival, succeeded him. Dryden, England's greatest literary figure, was now forced to give up his public offices and live by the proceeds of his pen alone.

Dryden was an excellent translator with his own style which brought the ire of many critics. Many felt he would embellish or expand anything he felt short or curt. Dryden did not feel such expansion was a fault, arguing that as Latin is a naturally concise language it cannot be duly represented by a comparable number of words in the much larger English vocabulary. He continued with his task of translating works by Horace, Juvenal, Ovid, Lucretius, and Theocritus, a task which he found far more satisfying than writing for the stage.

In 1694 he began work on what would be his most ambitious and defining work as translator, The Works of Virgil (1697), which was published by subscription. The publication of the translation of Virgil was a national event and brought Dryden the sum of £1,400.

His final translations appeared in the volume Fables Ancient and Modern (1700), a series of episodes from Homer, Ovid, and Boccaccio, as well as modernised adaptations from Geoffrey Chaucer interspersed with Dryden's own poems. As a translator, he made great literary works in the older languages available to readers of English.

John Dryden died on May 12th, 1700, and was initially buried in St. Anne's cemetery in Soho, before being exhumed and reburied in Westminster Abbey ten days later. He was the subject of poetic eulogies, such as Luctus Brittannici: or the Tears of the British Muses; for the Death of John Dryden, Esq. (London, 1700), and The Nine Muses.

He is seen as dominating the literary life of Restoration England to such a point that the period came to be known in literary circles as the Age of Dryden. Walter Scott called him "Glorious John."

Dryden was the dominant literary figure and influence of his age. He established the heroic couplet as a standard form of English poetry by writing successful satires, religious pieces, fables, epigrams, compliments, prologues, and plays with it; he also introduced the alexandrine and triplet into the form. In his poems, translations, and criticism, he established a poetic diction appropriate to the heroic couplet—Auden referred to him as "the master of the middle style"—that was a model for his contemporaries and for much of the 18th century. The considerable loss felt by the English literary community at his death was evident in the elegies written about him. Dryden's heroic couplet went on to become the dominant poetic form of the 18th century.

What Dryden achieved in his poetry was neither the emotional excitement of the early nineteenth-century romantics nor the intellectual complexities of the metaphysicals. Although he uses formal structures such as heroic couplets, he tried to recreate the natural rhythm of speech, and he knew that different subjects need different kinds of verse. In his preface to Religio Laici he says that "the expressions of a poem designed purely for instruction ought to be plain and natural, yet majestic... The florid, elevated and figurative way is for the passions; for (these) are begotten in the soul by showing the objects out of their true proportion.... A man is to be cheated into passion, but to be reasoned into truth."

Perhaps the following illustrates Dryden and his life—"The way I have taken, is not so streight as Metaphrase, nor so loose as Paraphrase: Some things too I have omitted, and sometimes added of my own. Yet the omissions I hope, are but of Circumstances, and such as wou'd have no grace in English; and the Addition, I also hope, are easily deduc'd from Virgil's Sense. They will seem (at least I have the Vanity to think so), not struck into him, but growing out of him".

Astraea Redux, 1660
The Wild Gallant (comedy), 1663
The Indian Emperour (tragedy), 1665
Annus Mirabilis (poem), 1667
The Enchanted Island (comedy), 1667, with William D'Avenant from Shakespeare's The Tempest
Secret Love, or The Maiden Queen, 1667
An Essay of Dramatick Poesie, 1668
An Evening's Love (comedy), 1668
Tyrannick Love (tragedy), 1669
The Conquest of Granada, 1670
The Assignation, or Love in a Nunnery, 1672
Marriage à la mode, 1672
Amboyna, or the Cruelties of the Dutch to the English Merchants, 1673
The Mistaken Husband (comedy), 1674
Aureng-zebe, 1675
All for Love, 1678
Oedipus (heroic drama), 1679, an adaptation with Nathaniel Lee of Sophocles' Oedipus
Absalom and Achitophel, 1681
The Spanish Fryar, 1681
Mac Flecknoe, 1682
The Medal, 1682
Religio Laici, 1682
To the Memory of Mr. Oldham, 1684
Threnodia Augustalis, 1685
The Hind and the Panther, 1687
A Song for St. Cecilia's Day, 1687
Britannia Rediviva, 1688, written to mark the birth of a Prince of Wales.
Amphitryon, 1690
Don Sebastian (play), 1690
Creator Spirit, by whose aid, 1690. Translation of Rabanus Maurus' Veni Creator Spiritus
King Arthur, 1691
Cleomenes, 1692
The Art of Satire, 1693
Love Triumphant, 1694
The Works of Virgil, 1697
Alexander's Feast, 1697
Fables, Ancient and Modern, 1700

www.ingramcontent.com/pod-product-compliance
Lightning Source LLC
Chambersburg PA
CBHW060143050426
42448CB00010B/2281